RED MIST

BY THE SAME AUTHOR

The History of Rain
Seatown

RED MIST

Roy Keane and the Football Civil War
A Fan's Story

Conor O'Callaghan

BLOOMSBURY

First published in Great Britain 2004

Copyright © 2004 by Conor O'Callaghan

The moral right of the author has been asserted

Bloomsbury Publishing Plc, 38 Soho Square, London W1D 3HB

Every reasonable effort has been made to contact copyright holders of
material reproduced in this book. If any have been inadvertently
overlooked, the publishers would be glad to hear from them and
to make good in future editions any errors or omissions brought to
their attention.

A CIP catalogue record for this book
is available from the British Library

ISBN 0 7475 7014 0

10 9 8 7 6 5 4 3 2

All papers used by Bloomsbury Publishing are natural,
recyclable products made from wood grown in
well-managed forests. The manufacturing processes conform
to the environmental regulations of the country of origin.

Typeset by Hewer Text Ltd, Edinburgh
Printed in Great Britain by Clays Ltd, St Ives plc

To Tommy, star of the show

Contents

Prologue

We begin in a B&B 3 miles outside a south-west market town, long after the story has finished. I am teaching primary school kids next day, and have been booked for one night into the Shanghai Select Accommodation and an evening meal with the other paying guests. The meal is fairly awkward. An Englishwoman at the other end of the table asks innocently what we all thought of Jack Charlton saying on last Friday's *Late Late Show* that Roy Keane should come back and play in next Saturday's showdown in Switzerland. The question, the company realises, has nothing to do with football. Silence. Directly opposite is a pair of middle-aged bachelor brothers. One has laid his cutlery to rest and the other is glancing nervously at him. The first brother says, 'That man is a traitor and a disgrace to his country.'

The other guests gaze at their place settings. They have witnessed too many suppers gone cold beneath this subject. They know, also, that the story is still too recent to find funny. I hear myself saying, 'Ah here . . . We all know the story inside out. I don't think any of us wants to go down that particular road tonight.'

The ladies present beam at me with gratitude. I feel like a hypocrite, but beam back all the same. I have spent the past year and a half actively picking scraps with all-comers on this very subject. My wife has booked babysitters and put on her glad rags only to find herself sitting alone in bars while her husband, gone up to buy a round, was still amid raised voices on the far side of the room an hour later. Now here I am, playing peacemaker, spiritual healer even. The landlady, who has been rooted to the spot with a tray of baked potatoes in her hands, puts an extra one on my plate.

'Thank you,' she says to me for all ears. 'Let us not have the Roy Keane row this once.'

I don't think, despite my recent politeness, that we actually know the story half as well as we think we do. What we know are only the story's bones. Roy Keane, Manchester United and Republic of Ireland captain, and the Republic of Ireland manager, Mick McCarthy, never got on. Keane was sent home from Ireland's 2002 World Cup squad after he and McCarthy had a big row. In the week that followed some people tried to get them to make up. Keane refused to say sorry and the Republic of Ireland, minus its captain, did better in the tournament than we all expected. Keane published a book at the end of the summer that broke all Irish bookselling records. After Ireland lost its first two matches of the Euro 2004 qualifying campaign, McCarthy resigned. The new manager asked Keane to come back. Keane said 'Yes', and then phoned the next day to say he meant 'No'.

With due respect to the dramatis personae, however, the story is not just about them. What happened on Saipan is only a tiny fraction of the narrative. Something else happened on the streets of Ireland in the week immediately after 23 May, and went on happening for the rest of 2002, that resembled a civil war. RTÉ's cameraman out there in the Pacific had a videophone only because he travelled directly from Kabul and never expected it to come out of its case. As it was, the videophone, borrowed by Sky and the BBC as well, saw more action during the World Cup than it had in Afghanistan. Grainy dawn reports from hotel roofs were beamed back to the screens of a nation in turmoil. Public protests were convened. Hits in one day on www.ireland.com, the website of the *Irish Times*, shattered all previous records, including September 11, 2001. Friendships ended. Political and religious leaders, ex-players, heartbroken millionaires, got involved. Social workers fielded calls, get-togethers were soured. A stuffed puppet turkey was admonished by seven year olds for remarks on kids' TV. A couple of senior football jobs were lost. Entries in letters pages of national newspapers and on cyber-polls became so voluminous and so heated as to make St Paul's Epistles to the Apostles seem positively reticent.

'What about the kids who'll never have a chance to play in a World Cup?' asked Tommy Gorman in the TV interview watched by almost one million speechless Irish men and women. Much of this book, more than he realises, I hope, is taken up with our football-mad seven year old, Tommy. It was his first World Cup. When the 23-man squad took off from Dublin Airport his favourite teddy was a rag doll named after the Irish captain. When the 22-man squad arrived back one month later he, along with most of the country, had temporarily blanked Roy Keane from his memory. I watched the story become part of his life: his heartbreak, his confusion and his faltering loyalties. I watched him being watched with impatience by his six-year-old sister, Eve. And eventually I watched the pair of them tiptoeing, bemused, around a father still struggling to come to terms with the story's fallout.

Before Korea/Japan 2002 the Republic of Ireland had played nine matches in World Cup Finals, scored five goals and managed only one actual victory in normal time. Despite those meagre stats, and because we were so delighted to have qualified at all, Mick McCarthy's predecessor Jack Charlton was fêted each time as a returning messiah. In the eight years since USA 1994, however, Ireland had modernised from being a borderline Third World nation to one of the wealthiest in Western Europe. Unemployment had halved. National aspirations had changed. A generation that had watched its parents drift through the motions of slapdash stage Irishry now aspired to a society rooted in work ethics and success. 'What makes this an epic drama rather than just another football tantrum,' Fintan O'Toole wrote in the *Guardian*, 'is that the row that prompted Keane's departure crystallises a cultural shift that is still in progress.'

Rewind. It is the end of the third week in May 2002. The Irish team has flown to a pre-tournament base of which few of us have ever heard. There have been rumours, our captain taking shortcuts through various journalists and lads out on the piss, but nothing out of the ordinary or important. Then one glorious Pacific evening, members of the Irish media entourage are eating pizza poolside when a breathless FAI lackey arrives with tidings. There will be an immediate unscheduled press conference in the Chinese restaurant of the team hotel next door. Reports reach home in time for the midday news. And at that point, the country we call 'Ireland' goes bananas.

PART I

Normal Time

It has been an extraordinary week. I have never
known one like it, in more than fifty years of
following the news in Ireland in the newspapers and
radio and television and private conversation.

Conor Cruise O'Brien,
Sunday Independent, 2 June 2002

I

I hear about it first on the afternoon of Wednesday, 22 May, at the new municipal swimming pool. I walk over to collect the kids, who go there once a week for lessons. Today, I feel boundlessly optimistic at the prospect of four weeks of football on the box. After the hooter goes, I have drifted over to the changing-room doors to help with shoes and wet hair and overhear two of the mums discussing the World Cup. I can't quite catch what they are saying. Then someone nearby momentarily switches off their hairdryer and the words 'Roy Keane' and 'disgrace' are audible in the pause.

I sidle over, last man on the planet to get wind of it. Roy had said he was going home. He cited 'personal reasons' and Colin Healy was called. Shortly before the final squad list was submitted to FIFA, Roy was persuaded to change his mind. One of the mums looks at me quizzically when I ask, 'But he's staying?'

'It's Colin Healy I feel sorry for,' she says as if I have completely missed the point. 'One day he's told he's going, and then the next day he's told he isn't.'

'But Roy *is* staying?'

'Oh, he's staying all right, now that he's got the attention he needed.'

She is a nice woman, and I am surprised to see her lip curled. Ordinarily, she strikes me as someone inclined to accentuate the positive, to see the best in people. She is one of those people who view life as something in which we all pull together, who takes a mums-and-toddlers-group mentality to just about everything, including the World Cup.

'If I had my way,' she says, 'he would have been sent home years ago.'

The squad has been in Saipan only five days. I raise a priggish you–don't–say eyebrow and she blushes from her boots up. She tries to mutter something like 'You know what I mean.' I feel like a bollocks for embarrassing her. But my overriding emotion is one of relief. Roy is still on course to play, and I contrived to miss the scary part of the drama.

Tommy and Eve know all about it; they tell me everything they have heard in sunlight on the pavement home. Eve says that Roy Keane was very bold. Her best friend said so. Tommy tells her to shut up. Parental obligation demands that I tick him off, but in truth he has said only what I wanted to say. I ask him what he heard. He says his best friend said that Roy and McCarthy are not talking to each other. Apart from that, he doesn't seem too worried. I take my cue from him, the way I do from airhostesses mid–flight: if they look happy, things must be okay. He asks me if Ireland ever won the World Cup before. I tell him that we haven't. To his seven-year-old ears, this is real news. He asks, 'Ever?'

'No.'

'But you do think we have a good chance this time?'

I smile. I can't say no, and yet I can't lie through my teeth either. My son is possibly only the second Irishman in history to think this thought. The first is currently marooned in a single hotel room out in the Pacific, and by the sounds of it wishes he wasn't.

2

Think of football as mutated tribalism. Once upon a century hilltop hamlets skirmished with their neighbours. Nowadays trainloads sing to and from away games under police supervision. That tribalism is a doddle if the club you follow is, say, a tube ride away from your childhood home. It also, in turn, seems to simplify your attitude to the national team: the national team comes a poor second. There's a funny bit in *Fever Pitch* where Nick Hornby describes 'what a miserable experience it is to go to Wembley to watch England play.' In *A Season With Verona*, Tim Parks befriends a season-ticket holder who is at every Hellas home game and yet is disinterested enough to go truffle-hunting when Italy is playing.

In Ireland, that kind of indifference would be unthinkable. The division of loyalty between club and country is an altogether more complicated affair. We support English clubs, which isn't unusual. Fans ferry weekly from here and Scandinavia (for that matter) and mainland Europe. But England, traditionally, is our old enemy. We are also, possibly, unique among football countries in that all the national squad's members play in foreign leagues. It has been twenty-four years since the semi-professional League of Ireland has yielded a player for the starting line-up of a competitive international. The clubs we follow and the players whose posters adorn our kids' walls all play in England or Scotland. As a result, our support for the national team is perhaps more emphatic than in other countries.

It wasn't always. In the dark ages BC (Before Charlton), when we were crap or were unable to translate a wealth of talent into qualification points, tickets for home games were as abundant on the streets of Dublin as nightclub vouchers midweek. Then Jack arrived on the scene, the team got places and for the first time touts considered it worth their while to loiter outside Landsdowne Road. What happened during the late eighties and early nineties, I think, was that the Republic of Ireland became our ideal club, like having our own Premier League team in Dublin. Ever since, all Irish fans have had two parallel teams about which they are equally passionate, two uses of the collective 'we'.

3

My wife brings home a newspaper. She works part time in the local college and gets them at student rates. So I usually wait until the evening when the news is already completely out of date. This evening I am on the doorstep before she has activated the car alarm. She seems flattered that her arrival should be a source of such excitement, more so when I offer to carry her bags.

Roy is front page, tossing a bottle of still water past Packie Bonner's shoulder. It seems the squad arrived at its pre-tournament base on the Pacific island of Saipan to find no kit or balls and a bumpy pitch. Yesterday, at training, Roy objected to the fact that the three goalkeepers were excused from the end-of-session match. He quarrelled with Bonner, McCarthy's assistant Ian Evans, and reserve keeper Alan Kelly. When they got back to the hotel, he spoke to McCarthy under a parasol in the hotel grounds and expressed a wish to go home. Celtic midfielder Colin Healy was tracked down at his family home in Ballincolig, Co. Cork, and told he was on. At some point during the night his family, his agent Michael Kennedy and his manager at United, Alex Ferguson, persuaded Roy to change his mind. In the wee hours of this morning our time, the squad list including his name was faxed to FIFA with ten minutes' leeway.

I flick on *The Last Word*, the top-rating drive-time radio show hosted by Eamon Dunphy, ghost of Roy's forthcoming autobiography. Johnny Giles is on. Giles had been Ireland player/manager to Dunphy in the seventies. They are also the resident panellists on *The Premiership* on RTÉ. From a distance they have always seemed close. Now here they are on the national airwaves, bickering like starlings. Giles has an article in this evening's *Evening Herald*, arguing that McCarthy should not have accepted Roy back into the squad. Dunphy deems this 'a disgraceful attack on a great player'. It's bitter, unlistenable stuff. My wife says, 'Is this as serious as it sounds?'

'Nah,' I bluff, 'it'll be grand.'

'They were all talking about it up in the college.'

'Were they?'

'A lot of long faces in the canteen.'

'Really?'

When I go in to kiss Tommy goodnight, he is sitting up in the top bunk. He asks me if we are still going to win the World Cup. I tell him that we are. Then he says, 'I wish Denis Irwin was out there.'

He means Roy's fellow Corkman and United colleague, retired from international duty two years ago. Up until then they roomed together, now Roy rooms alone. I had no idea Tommy even knew Denis existed. It transpires the sentiments were overheard from the school caretaker. I laugh and he is embarrassed. I tell him it will be grand. After my wife hits the sack, I go online. There have been no advances. The sentries have heard nothing untoward rustling out in the darkness. This, I assume, is the good news that comes as no news and hit Disconnect.

4

'We' hadn't qualified for a major tournament since USA 1994. We had lost a play-off with Holland for England 1996 and Jack Charlton went fishing, permanently. His successor, Mick McCarthy, had watched his team surrender a place in France 1998 to a Belgium team that in turn was eliminated by South Korea. We had blown, in the most painful fashion imaginable, the automatic slot for Holland/Belgium 2000 in the group that included Croatia and Yugoslavia.

We were drawn in the same qualifying group as two of the pre-tournament favourites for Korea/Japan 2002, and nobody was giving us a prayer.

Holland away, 2 September 2000. We were out west, in my wife's family's summerhouse, eking out the last drops of the summer. We were two up after seventy and clung on for a point. Out of blind fury, I decided the sitting room needed a lick of paint, and set to masking there and then. The phone started ringing before the echo of the ref's whistle had faded.

'Sickener.'

'Sickener.'

'What we have we hold. The Irish way.'

'Goodnight.'

Portugal away, a month later. Matt Holland, a player of whom we had never heard, levelled it with ten minutes left. There is still a spring broken in the armchair in our sitting room and I have watched all subsequent internationals from the edge of the coffee table. Estonia at home the following Wednesday; 2–0 and a bizarre stat in my son's World Cup sticker book that says Robbie Keane was replaced by 'Foley'.

'Is Foley good?'

'He's an excellent player,' I say.

'You've never heard of him, have you?'

'No.'

Cyprus, March 2001. The literary festival of which I was director was in full swing and I got the half-time score from the theatre porters. The second half was on the big screen in the pub where I, between events, entertained two famous English writers who shall remain nameless. They both despised football and said so upon entering the premises. My contribution to the conversation was vague, and involved a lot of humming and pensive gazing into the distance. I excused myself on a bogus call of nature and asked some Dub with a scarf tied around his head, 'Final score?'

'Four-nil.'

'Good?'

'Brutal.'

'How did we win four-nil if we were brutal?'

'Roy Keane.'

Back-to-back conquests of Andorra. David Connolly was substituted, uninjured, in the twenty-sixth minute of the first game. We'd be in Barcelona yet, trying to open our account, if our captain hadn't persuaded their keeper to topple him in the area. For two whole minutes of the second match they had the lead and the nation sat in silent panic, thinking about banana skins. A draw with Portugal at home on 2 June. One of those sunny Landsdowne afternoons when our centre backs Steven Staunton and Richard Dunne became Laurel and Hardy, and Roy seemed not so much a footballer as a force-field. His demolition job on Alfie Haaland in the Manchester derby had ended his club season prematurely. He looked rested. He scored. After the game Eusebio came into our dressing room to request his jersey. Roy also got a yellow card for bitching at the ref and missed the win in Estonia four days later.

Holland at home, 1 September 2001. We watched it in the pub nearest our family home, opposite the train station. Just before kick-off, members of a wedding-bound showband, in on the Dublin express, appeared inside the side door in dress suits. The double-bass player was a bearded pudding with a voice like thunder. He was also an archetypal Roy-hater. There are always a few and they tend to be vocal. When the camera passed our captain during the national anthem, he bellowed sarcastically, 'Nice of you to turn up!'

Roy upended Marc Overmars inside sixty seconds.

'Send him off ref,' roared Showband Seamus. 'Teach the bollocks a lesson!'

That was exactly 364 days after the 2–2 draw in the Amsterdam Arena – one for every chance Holland missed at Landsdowne Road. Down to ten, Jason McAteer scored our one chance. I said to the guy sitting next to me, 'That's the equaliser' and the showband left. Tommy was waiting for me on the front wall and I was 'nicely' (that uniquely Irish euphemism for 'drunk'). He was wearing the only green top in his wardrobe, a Teenage Mutant Ninja Turtle T-shirt. I fell asleep on his beanbag on the sitting-room floor. He had videoed the whole game. For a few weeks we sat on the edge of the coffee table together, watching McAteer's goal to the end of the third slow-motion replay and then holding a thumb on the Rewind button until they had all backpedalled to the point where Ian Harte was about to feed Roy on the left touchline. My wife would appear now and then at the partition doors and plead, 'Can we turn that off for a while?'

'Just one more time,' Tommy would say.

In our 4–0 home win over Cyprus a fortnight later, striker David Connolly did something that you suspected even he had given up on. He struck.

November 2001. We watched the first leg of the play-off with Iran in our brother's local in Kerry. That we won 2–0 and our keeper Shay Given was given man-of-the-match tells its own story. The following morning we turned on Sky News to hear that Roy had flown back to Manchester with a swollen knee and wouldn't be travelling to Tehran. He watched the second leg at home. He was, by his own admission, 'flicking'.

I was teaching poetry to eight year olds in south Dublin four days later. We wrote a collective 'Prayer for the Boys in Green' on the blackboard and shouted it aloud together. I forgot it was a non-denominational school and was treated to a gentle lecture at the coffee break. The match was on in the car on the way home. The presenter, Joe Duffy, described significant events as they happened on his monitor and filled in the boring bits by chatting to obscure celebs in the studio about their earliest, funniest football memories. I was screaming at the radio. At one point, gridlocked at the airport coming out of Dublin, a taxi driver gridlocked alongside me in the other direction rolled down his window.

'You wouldn't read about it,' he was roaring. 'The most important game in the history of Irish football and all we can get is some gobshite talking about his mammy.'

I caught the final twenty minutes on the edge of the coffee table. The locals were throwing sticks onto the pitch. Where did they get the sticks? Then Iran scored in injury time and the word 'Skopje' flitted across my mind. In Skopje in October 1999 we conceded a 94th-minute equaliser in the last qualifier for Euro 2000. Niall Quinn had caught up with Frank Stapleton's record in the first half, but Roy was injured again and we couldn't put them away. The last ten minutes was one of those passages of play only Eastern Europe throws up. Our legs were gone and the home crowd, 'sensing something' as summarisers always phrase it, began to make serious noise. They were awarded a corner in the fourth minute of injury time, even though the fourth official had held aloft a fairly obvious '3'. Any Irish fan can still pronounce and spell the name of the sub whose header cost us an automatic slot: Goran Staverevsks. To this day the Irish squad have a yellow jersey that's awarded to the worst trainer of any given session. They call it 'The Macedonia'.

Just as Iran were pressing forward again and I seriously began believing I was having a coronary, the ref blew. We won. Or rather, we lost 1–0 but went through all the same. All the neighbours were standing on their doorsteps, congratulating one another the way they do at New Year. A couple of freight ships over in the port were taking long pulls of their foghorns as if their foghorns were Cuban cigars. You could hear cars beeping up the town. Our phone rang inside. It was my younger brother. The conversation in its entirety ran:

Him: 'I thought it was another Macedonia.'

Me: 'I think we all did.'

Him: 'But it wasn't.'

Me: 'No, it wasn't.'
Him: 'The World Cup.'
Me: 'The World Cup.'

5

The morning of 23 May, a Thursday that henceforth we shall call *the* Thursday. The kids have gone to school and I can't really settle at the screen. The radio says there's an interview with Roy in the *Irish Times* in which he's critical of the FAI. 'And this is news?' I say rhetorically to the corner of the room. I waste a couple of hours listening to CDs. I go uptown, without my wallet or anybody to meet. I talk to the lollipop man who mans the school at the end of our road. He is just donning his luminous bib for the tots' early lunchtime traffic. He must be pushing seventy. He's famous for being the lollipop man who warns heedless drivers with yellow and red cards flashed into their rear-view mirrors. He's a big United fan and we usually slag a bit. There is one subject on which we agree and this morning there is no slagging.

'He's not a happy camper,' he says.

'Stop.'

'McCarthy hasn't a clue.'

'Stop.'

'What do you think happened, Liverpool?'

We don't know each other's name. Instead, we have labelled one another with monickers that make us sound like Navajo braves. He knows I support Liverpool so he calls me 'Liverpool'. I think of him as 'Small World' because of his insistent and consistent misuse of that phrase. I never call him it to his face, only to my wife on those very rare occasions when Small World enters the nightly narrative of the kinds of day we've had.

'I don't know,' I say. 'I don't think any of us will ever really know.'

'Ah c'mon Liverpool, your head's in the sand.'

'Maybe.'

'Small world, you know?'

'*What?*'

I go into a shop uptown that belongs to the older brother of someone I used be close to at school. It's the only place on earth where I get addressed as Mister. The guy can't remember my christian name, but has the wit to pitch it as deference. I set my heart on a pair of beige canvas drawstrings and draw the curtain of the fitting unit. I have the shorts I left the house in around my ankles when the DJ cuts across the music on the speakers and says something like, 'Sorry to interrupt folks, but we're going straight over to the sports desk for some news you ain't gonna enjoy.'

They say everyone in Ireland remembers where they were the moment John F. Kennedy was assassinated in Dallas. They say it's the fact that he was the first president with an Irish Catholic background. Whatever the reason, there's a whole generation of wrinklies who can tell you precisely their longitude and latitude on the afternoon of 22 November 1963. My mother, for example, was giving birth to our eldest brother. Suddenly all these nuns were on their knees in the delivery ward, launching into a decade of the rosary. My mother says she scandalised the penguins by screaming, 'I wish somebody would bloody shoot me.'

Then the music fades back up and I start groaning.

'No, Nooo . . .'

A hesitant voice appears the far side of the curtain, as if the fitting unit were a confessional.

'Everything a.o.k. in there, Mr O'Callaghan?'

'No.'

My shorts are still resting around my sandals.

'Anything I can do to help?'
'NO!'

6

Beneath the national euphoria of qualification, we all knew, lay a
bundle of troubling truths. Captain and manager, for example,
disliked each other. There is a much-repeated story about a
contretemps they had at the end of the US Cup in 1992. It was
Roy's first tour with the national squad and Mick's last as a player.
Roy was last to board, three sheets to the wind. Mick asked him if
he considered his behaviour befitting of a professional footballer,
and Roy in response asked if Mick considered his first touch
befitting of a professional footballer. In 1996, during McCarthy's
first game as Irish manager, Roy became the youngest ever captain
of the Irish senior team and was also sent off. As he left he whipped
the armband from his sleeve and threw it towards the bench.

Partly through absenting himself in controversial circumstances
from the summer tour of America in 1996, partly through surgery
on his knee, and partly through a one-match suspension, Roy
missed our next nine internationals. On his return as sweeper against
Iceland in November he was rewarded with another more dubious
accolade: the first Irish player in living memory to be at the wrong
end of an orchestrated booing by the home fans. Cathal Dervan,
ghost of Mick's forthcoming World Cup diary, had urged the
crowd to 'let him know what you think' and Roy hasn't forgotten.

Old stories and old grievances we hoped had been laid to rest by
the time qualification for Korea/Japan came around. Roy had been
reinstated as captain in 1998, and he and McCarthy seemed to learn
to tolerate one another in the belief that each wanted the same
thing. Then, after the 2–2 draw with Holland in September 2000,

cracks began to reappear. McCarthy dashed onto the pitch to congratulate his men and the captain bitched in the tunnel to the press about setting higher standards, actually winning. After our win in Cyprus, Roy slammed the amateurism of the FAI and said he was considering quitting. Gradually, he reported later and later for international duty and communicated with McCarthy only via Mick Byrne, the squad's assistant physio. When the team travelled to Tallinn without its captain, a number of players confessed that they were sick of being described as a one-man team.

During those fifteen months of qualification from September 2000, Roy's mind was clearly on other matters. The all-conquering Manchester United team he also captained was imploding, much to his vocal frustration. There were reports in the press that he was being treated for alcohol-related depression, although he denied this. When he walked off the Landsdowne Road pitch after our win over Holland, the man-of-the-match looked like someone stepping from the wreckage of a car crash in which his family had been killed. The manager was clearly losing patience with the credit being afforded his captain. He elected Steven Staunton as his player of the qualifying campaign, even though Staunton had started only four of our ten group matches. He peevishly told the people of Tehran had they could call his team the 'Republic of Roy Keane' for all he cared. There were rumours among the players after that match that Roy had never bothered to get a visa to Iran, and more than a few raised eyebrows when his swollen knee had recovered sufficiently for him to play against Leicester in the Premiership the following weekend.

Ten minutes after the final whistle of the second leg of the play-off in Tehran, I took the kids over the road to buy celebratory choc ices. Gerry, a big United fan who works behind the counter, had a portable up where the nappy boxes normally are and I was full of the joys.

'Just as long as Roy travels,' Gerry was saying.

'What do you mean?'

'I mean if Roy travels, we'll be okay. If he doesn't . . .'

'Why wouldn't he?'

I bought the papers that weekend, the way you always do after the success of a big game, to read nice things about your team. Tom Humphries, the thinking man's football guru in the *Irish Times*, gave a qualification overview. His praise of Roy was underscored by a worried and worrying foreboding. I tried not to envisage the implications. But from that moment a dark cloud, with no noticeable silver lining, had appeared on my horizon and was getting closer:

The players will refuse to publicly discuss Roy . . . This team hardly makes it onto Roy's Christmas card list. He is so solitary that one wonders if he has any such list. Yet his will runs right through this team. They fear him, love him, loathe him, mainly they voyage around him. Next summer they'll get to spend four or five weeks with him.

7

The spectator's fate – we watch but in the end we have to guess
Ian Hamilton, *Gazza Agonistes*

I am seated on the edge of the coffee table, gaping at the one o'clock news on the telly. There is no footage. Saipan is so remote that it hasn't a satellite link. All tapes have to been carrier-pigeoned to a neighbouring island and beamed from there. George Hamilton, RTÉ's equivalent of John Motson, is plugging the void in studio. I am screaming, 'What happened?' It seems there was some sort of team meeting convened to discuss the *Irish Times* interview. Mick called a press conference immediately after, and used the term 'slanging match'. The captain has been formally expelled from the squad.

George is hedging his bets. He appears as much in the dark as the rest of us. He accepts that a player, even one of Roy's stature, cannot expect to be able to criticise both manager and governing body and yet remain a party to the World Cup party. On the other hand, prophetically, he says if this proves another example of the FAI's bargain-basement attitude to preparation, it will be very expensive in the long run.

I trudge across the road to view the *Irish Times* for myself. Gerry is in the thick of the lunchtime trade. Today, for once, the sight of a hundred miniskirts from the girls' secondary school does nothing for either of us. I am rifling through the news-stand when I catch his eye. We shake disbelieving heads in unison. I go up when the number of girls, blissfully oblivious to just how nigh the world's end is, has thinned. Gerry has his elbow on the till and is rubbing his forehead. He looks like someone who has just been informed of his father's death, but who has manfully elected to labour through his grief. He nods disapprovingly at my choice of reading.

'Don't know how you can bring yourself to buy that.'

'I have to read it for myself,' I say.

Peter's solution is nothing if not direct.

'Boycott the *Times* and shoot McCarthy.'

'Give me a shotgun and I'll gladly do the second bit.'

'Join the queue, kid.'

I spread the interview on the kitchen table. Roy is talking about why he missed Niall's testimonial, his refusal to collaborate on a programme note with Cathal Dervan, the bust-up on the training ground with the goalkeepers, his decision and u-turn about coming home. Sure, there is some vaguely critical stuff about the logistics. But no names and nothing too damning. You wonder what got through to McCarthy. Is it the reference to Roy's manager at

United: 'the only person I would listen to'? If it is, then Mick must have an even thinner skin than we imagined. The references, however, to the rest of the Irish team are darker: 'Some people accept it easier. Maybe that's why some of our players are playing where they are.' Those words alone put paid to any backing Roy could have hoped for from his colleagues.

But none of it is untrue or, more importantly, uninteresting. It is also only a fraction of what is a marvellously candid anatomy of the human frailty behind sporting stats, the kind of chat you never hear from footballers. Roy refers to his image as 'the monster'. He talks about being alone in his hotel room, missing his kids, getting depressed and yet learning to live with himself. He seems painfully aware of the distance between himself and the rest of the squad. At the very end, Tom Humphries asks him about being Irish manager in the future. Roy's response, a customary dig at himself, is both funny and sad. 'Yeah,' he replies, 'nobody would play for me but we'd have great facilities!'

The only scoop is Roy's insistence that Korea/Japan will end his international career. The whole interview is imbued with a battle-worn 'when all this is over' wistfulness. It is credit to Humphries' skill as an interviewer that he manages to get Roy to a point where he feels relaxed enough to ramble. He talks about quitting football altogether, of 'summers in Australia, doing courses'. It's an irresistible image: Keano swatting flies down under, his own restaurant and a pot belly, teaching himself Italian and generally basking in blissful anonymity.

The phone goes.

'Mr O'Callaghan?'

'Yes?'

It is the principal of Tommy and Eve's school, twenty minutes after bell-time. She is laughing.

'Shit! I'm on my way.'

My arrival is almost half an hour after the final bell, but there are still lots of cars in the yard. It's like 9/11 all over again. I tell them on the way home and this time Tommy hasn't heard.

'What happened?'

'Roy and McCarthy had a big row, and Roy got sent home.'

'Why didn't Mick get sent home?'

'Because Mick's the manager.'

'Yeah, but he's not the boss. Not really.'

His disgust at his old man for being so late gives way to silence. Then on the front doorstep he asks for further clarification. I think my answer serves only to complicate the issue further in his head.

'And now he's coming home?'

'Yeah.'

'To Ireland?'

'Well, to England.'

8

I blame myself. Supporting a team depends on the illusion that you too are involved. It's not merely a question of contributing to the volume on the terraces and waving inflatable shamrocks. It is more often the silent private superstitions observed in the fallow days between games, the football-free months between seasons, that make the difference. It's a neurotic, exclusively negative power. You never think you can help your team to win, but one unlucky barstool sat upon or one wrong notion admitted across your train of thought, and it's all your fault.

Now that it has happened I realise that the whole country has been living in dread of this for seven months. When Roy pulled his hamstring away to Deportivo La Coruna last April, you could almost feel a collective heartbeat being missed. Even those of us who supported United's sworn enemies, mindful of the captain's good spirits, winced silently when they lifted neither the title nor the Champions' League. I had utterly zoned out of the World Cup experience in the run-up. I think I believed, subconsciously, that if I somehow managed to be indifferent then the whole shebang would run like clockwork. I even contemplated not watching a single game, or at least not live. I had this daft daydreamt scheme whereby they would be taped as live on my behalf and watched in the haze of July. The rationale being that the one time I didn't care we would surely go all the way.

I took only a passing interest when Roy was awarded his honorary doctorate by the National University of Ireland, Cork, on 10 May. Niall's testimonial, and the furore in a teacup over Roy's no-show, passed me by. I paid no heed to the filthy 'friendly' against Nigeria, immediately before flying out. I managed, for the first time in living memory, to immerse myself in my democratic rights on polling day. I became so versed in the nuances of proportional representation that I was completely unaware of the mayhem surrounding their send-off in Dublin Airport. And my head was buried so deep in sand that I had to be told about the captain's tantrum and u-turn by the Jesus-loving, scout-supervising mum of one of our seven-year-old son's school chums.

After that, the damage had been done. There is still part of me that feels that if I could have kept it at arm's length a wee while longer, everything would have turned out sweet. But I couldn't resist checking the net that night, fretting like a duck in thunder, lest any further news had broken through. I had to confer with my amused wife at breakfast the next day. I had to share a frank exchange of views with the lollipop man. I had to go up the town to see what the hoi polloi were making of it. And most of all, I had go into the only local clothes shop I frequent. I had to try something on. I couldn't ignore the radio, could I? After that, the sky fell in.

9

'Slightly better!'

The words I am spitting at the telly are Mick McCarthy's, uttered in footage on the six o'clock news from the press conference in Saipan: 'We're a good side, *slightly better* with him in it than when he's not.' Mick is seated at a round table. His face is pale grey. Niall Quinn is there, Steven Staunton, Alan Kelly and somebody from the Football Association of Ireland. There is a lot of jowl-stroking and sighing. It's difficult to make out exactly what happened. Mick is saying:

> I called a meeting and I asked anybody, certainly Roy, to make his comments rationally and logically, and that didn't happen. I'm afraid that it turned into a bit of a slanging match and I'm afraid I cannot and will not tolerate being spoken to with that level of abuse thrown at me, so I sent him home.

Tommy has spent the last three hours at the desk in his bedroom, drawing pictures of Ireland jerseys with number six on them. When the news started up, I called from the bottom of the stairs to test the water and down he trudged. We have been on the edge of the coffee table ever since. His mother asks him if his homework is done and I apologise. I suggest giving our son a note for the morning. She is not impressed.

'What will the note say? "Dear teacher, Tommy couldn't do his homework last night because Roy Keane was thrown out of the World Cup"?'

Steven Staunton, pride of our home town of Dundalk, describes what happened as 'unacceptable' and talks at length about lines. He has taken over as captain. Niall Quinn confirms his 'complete allegiance to Mick'. Alan Kelly, the reserve keeper who quarrelled with Keane on Tuesday, 'never witnessed anything like it'. Pundits and ex-players row in with interchangeable opinions and we, literally, switch off. I go out for pints with two of my brothers after the motions of tea, homework and bed are gone through. The place is black but very quiet. It's like a wake. Everybody seems to be discussing the same thing. There are whole minutes of silence between us, broken only by expletives or disbelieving laughs as our respective trains of thought surface back at the same point. We skip the customary fourth. On the late news at home RTÉ's sports editor, Tony O'Donoghue, is on the videophone from the roof of Dai Ichi Hotel, where it is almost dawn. Tony says the team will be waking soon and flying to Japan.

Friday the 24th is the first ever morning I buy the newspapers with a credit card. It comes to almost €20. Each rag has at least one detail the others missed. Keane had breakfast with the rest of the team. They trained from ten until half past twelve and the captain was, according to one paper, 'surprisingly cheerful'. McCarthy spoke to the press at lunchtime and insisted that events of the past two days were over. In the afternoon, most of the squad played head-tennis on the beach and Roy gave interviews both to RTÉ radio and TV. Word of the *Irish Times* piece, its ink still drying, started to rumble through. McCarthy was asked to comment on his captain's retirement announcement. It was news to him. Roy whiled away the late afternoon on the beach behind the Hyatt, sunbathing and chatting with the team doctor.

The players sat to dinner in the hotel ballroom at 6.30 in the knowledge that the manager wished to speak to them at 7.30. In the intervening hour, somebody kindly printed off the interview from the *Irish Times* website and gave it to McCarthy. When McCarthy spoke, he invited his captain to air any grievances and found himself at the receiving end of a dressing-down which lasted somewhere between five and twelve minutes, depending on which paper you read. All reports agree, however, the words 'f★★king w★★ker' featured. After Roy left the room, the team applauded the manager. At nine o'clock the press were called to the Chinese restaurant, while a string quartet warbled in the foyer. The full text of what Mick told them in those ten minutes is reprinted ad nauseam. What stands out is the amount of uses of the phrase 'I'm afraid', but no amount of annotation will convey his frightened pause between 'I' and 'sent'.

The most surprising aspect to reaction from the game's thinkers is the complete absence of surprise. Mark Lawrenson, former Ireland and Liverpool all-star and current BBC pundit, tells the *Irish Times*: 'To be honest, I wasn't stunned by the news . . . I almost think that when Roy got to Saipan he realised he didn't want to be there.' Over in *The Times* James Lawton, who deems Roy's actions 'an assault on the spirit of the game', writes: 'Keane's departure is a sadness, and none the less because it became so inevitable.' In the same paper, Simon Barnes reckons Roy 'has behaved like a fool and . . . a pig'. By contrast Tom Humphries, the man whose interview opened the final act, describes someone 'capable of immense warmth and loyalty, flashes of high good humour and generosity'. In the *Daily Telegraph* Henry Winter condemns 'an intelligent but complicated individual'. His colleague Paul Hayward heralds 'a significant defeat for [sic] the rampaging ego'. Ex-players, sports psychologists, Cork publicans, an expert on male conflict resolution, prophets of economic doom are all consigned to the recycle bin by lunch.

The team has already flown to Japan. Last night a few of them dropped in to room 758 to say sayonara and found their *ex*-captain happier than he had been all week. On the plane out of Saipan he was the butt of all their jokes. Someone even spotted a dot and shouted, 'Look lads, there's Roy!' and the squad cracked up. Back at the Hyatt, waiting for a 4pm departure, Roy was slamming the receiver on all journalists. A trio of adventurers managed to slip through the lift's security code for the seventh floor, sweet talk the heavy manning the corridor, and knocked on Roy's door. He stuck his head out, smiling and just out of the shower, and promised an exclusive in the foyer in ten minutes. The hotel manager, however, had other ideas. As a decoy, a limo and empty baggage were lined at the front door while Roy boarded a courtesy van out the back. There ensued a surreal car chase to the airport at 30mph, the strictly enforced island speed limit. Now there he is on the lunchtime news, in unofficial casuals, queuing to check in beside the Exit sign. 'I'm feeling absolutely great,' he is saying. 'I have absolutely no regrets about anything.'

10

An affable Irregular,
A heavily-built Falstaffian man,
Comes cracking jokes of civil war
As though to die by gunshot were
The finest play under the sun.

W.B. Yeats, 'The Road at My Door'

The day after the expulsion from paradise, the parcel postman arrives with a book on Japanese soccer for me to review for the *Irish Times*. He has left the driver's door on his van hanging open and I can hear his radio.

'Well,' I say, 'what are they saying now?'

He leans against the door frame and grimaces.

'Paul McGrath is on with Pat Kenny,' he says. 'He reckons it's a national disaster, a state of emergency.'

'What do you reckon?'

'Oh, an ambush. An old-style civil war ambush.'

He laughs.

'Meet us at the crossroads and we'll give you a surprise for your years of service.'

He closes his eyes and taps an index finger against one of his temples.

'Dot dot dot.'

II

Tommy has been grilling his old man with starters-for-ten pertaining specifically to East Asian geography. Truth to tell, I haven't the foggiest where Saipan is, although since all this has happened we have had no option but to become authorities on its recent history.

I have a brainwave to deflect away all unanswerable questions. Instead of a bedtime story, we sit on the toy trunk – me, Tommy, Eve – and see if we can find Saipan in the *Philip's World Atlas*. We think it will be a doddle. We think all we have to do is open it at the page and there will be Japan with our spot beside it like a pimple on an orange. No. Japan has its own Milky Way of islands. Trying to locate Saipan reminds me of the night in winter we stood out the back in our anoraks and hats, with a book on astronomy and a torch, trying to pinpoint one star in a zillion.

There are a thousand minute amorphous green shapes surrounded by the duck-egg blue of the shallow Pacific. Tommy starts reading aloud their names. The stilted litany takes on the air of a mid-century catechism said from memory in Latin.

'Kuchino-Shima. Nakano-Shima. Suwanose-Jima. Akuseki-Shima. Oki-Shotō. Sado. Rishiri-Tō. Tok Do. Kobi-Sho. Uji-Guntō. Yoron-Jima. Ullung Do.'

We are getting nowhere. Eve says she is bored. She has had

enough of 'stupid Roy Keane' and turns in on the lower bunk, accompanied by an unfilled hot-water bottle called Alice. I try a different tack. Forget Saipan. Instead, we get the globe and attempt to map Roy's flight path to Manchester. It is estimated to take twelve hours direct, and Saipan is nine hours ahead of us. Hard sums. In the absence of pictures of him arriving in Manchester, knackered, we figure he is still up there somewhere.

Tommy closes his eyes and drops a pencil into the blue beneath the southernmost tip. Just like that, he creates a whole new island in our atlas, much as the spat between Roy and Mick has created a place that hitherto didn't exist in the Irish imagination. I take the wheel to start with. I imagine travelling due north, the way they do on trans-Atlantic flights. Leaving the grey squiggle, I steer it up over Hiroshima and make a straight line as the crow flies towards Vladivostok.

'Does the Yellow Sea really have yellow water?'

'Shush. You're disturbing the pilot.'

Tommy insists on taking over. He negotiates a sharp left-hander just as we reach that coastal tip at which the borders of Russia and China and North Korea meet, like slices on a pie-chart. He likes the Gobi Desert, the name, the idea of it. His driving is more erratic than mine. He drifts south, hugging the hard shoulder of the Himalayan Plateau, its purple and flecks of white. We chat about yaks and altitude sickness. I chance a leading question.

'Does the pilot fancy putting his head down in the back?'

'Nah. You can if you want.'

'Tajikistan.'

'What?'

'The next country's Tajikistan.'

'Oh.'

'Were you ever there?'

'What?'

He is giggling.

'Were you ever there?'

'Where?'

'Tajikistan.'

'God yeah.'

'When?'

'What?'

'WHEN?'

'Years ago.'

'Before I was born?'

'That's right. Before you were born. Anyway, I'm there now again, aren't I? Eyes on the road, please.'

Samarkand. The Caspian Sea. Tbilisi. The Black Sea. Odessa. Vienna. Paris. Just as we reach the coast of Normandy, Tommy starts to wilt. I lift him into the top bunk. Eve is half asleep and whimpering. Her brother is losing altitude. Only going down the stairs do I remember Roy. We have abandoned him mid-air, in darkness, somewhere out there above the English Channel.

12

There was an odd moment at a press conference in Tehran last November. McCarthy was being quizzed about the forthcoming play-off second leg. A local reporter raised a hesitant hand and asked if Mick could discuss whether or not his Englishness got in the way in an Irish dressing room. Silence. A few of the visiting reporters shut their eyes and slunk into their chairs, waiting for gunfire. After an age, during which Mick fixed the questioner with a contemptuous gaze, he said:

Say if your father left Iran because he couldn't get work at home, and he ended up going to England where there was lots. And say if your father had a son who grew up in England, speaking English with an English accent. Now, does that mean the boy isn't entitled to call himself Iranian?

The morning of 25 May, the Saturday. It now seems an irrefutable fact that Roy called Mick an 'English c★★t' during the team meeting. Roy will deny this several times over in the coming year, but all this morning's papers say it's so. In truth, ever since the introduction of the 'Granny Rule' that qualified foreign-born players with Irish parents or grandparents to tog out in green, this is the delicate dormant subject around which all Ireland has tiptoed for years. Now it has exploded in our faces.

Even Tom Humphries, the journalist so loyal that you suspect he would defend Roy's actions for a late tackle from behind on Mrs Humphries, writes in this morning's *Irish Times*: 'There were shocked whispers afterwards that Keane had questioned McCarthy's Irishness, a tack that would instantly have alienated him from half the squad.' According to the *Daily Mirror*'s reporter the thirteen members of the Irish squad, whose 'hearts are as big and as Irish as their shamed former captain's', were 'personally offended'. A government source told the *Star* that the Taoiseach, Bertie Ahern, was originally prepared to mediate in the row, but that now he has backed off after learning the full extent of what the insider calls 'such vicious abuse and such horrific language'. Andy Townsend went on the radio yesterday and suggested that Roy would have been safer simply hitting Mick than casting aspersions on his nationality. Then Jack Charlton appeared last night on *The Late Late Show*, the nation's favourite chat show, and criticised Roy's actions and Paul McGrath's defence. He also gave a tour de force in the role of shocked ingénue. Jack, or so the story went, had been standing on a riverbank for the past week and wasn't up to speed. To spare the delicate ears of the studio audience, host Pat Kenny handed over a clipboard with the words written on it. Jack's brow creased. 'I would have got hold of him and thrown him out the door,' he shouted. 'That's disgraceful. You don't do things like that.'

The *Sun* is advertising an actor's censored reconstruction of the 'full torrent of filth fired at the boss'. For 32c a minute you can 'Hear Roy's Rant'. The wording that appears in the *Daily Mirror* is depressingly consistent throughout the papers. What he said was:

> The only reasons I have any dealings with you is that somehow you are the manager of my country & you're not even Irish you English c★★t. You can stick it up your b★★★★★★s.

The front pages are littered with asterisks. They make the breakfast table look like stills of a blizzard. I say this to my wife sitting opposite in her dressing gown. She doesn't laugh or smile. She knows me enough to know this is hurting much more than I can admit. Little did we realise how fortunate we were with 'f★★king w★★ker'. Now this. Eve puts her index finger under 'c★★t' and asks, 'What does that spell?'

'Guess.'

'Coat?'

'That's right. Coat.'

'And that?'

'Guess.'

'Too hard.'

'C'mon.'

'Bananas.'

'Very good.'

Tommy, too old and too cute to be fooled, starts giggling.

'Roy Keane called Mick McCarthy "an English coat", and told him to "stick the World Cup up his bananas"?'

'That's right.'

We all laugh.

'It isn't that though, Dad, is it?'

'No.'

13

Ireland's Secret Formula: Find an island with a red light zone but no soccer pitch, go on binges and send your best player home.

Daily Mail, 25 May 2002

The barber on the square I go to once a fortnight, Benny, is a big Liverpool fan as well. He is delighted Keane was sent home. We have an animated but fairly good-humoured discussion as he brushes me down.

'He had it coming,' Benny says.

'He got them there, Benny.'

'Bullshit. Football is an eleven-man game. Keane's fatal error was that he forgot that.'

Unlike yours truly, Benny actually plays for a local club in the winter league. He sees recent events as a victory for the honest footsoldier over the pampered officer, a long-overdue lesson for prima donnas everywhere. I have never seen Benny so articulate, so full of beans. Usually, he is little more than a sequence of hungover grunts. The late afternoon of the 25th he is whistling.

'I'm surprised at you,' he says. 'I thought you were Liverpool.'

'I am, but when Roy puts on the green jersey . . .'

'He's a tramp, Man U scum.'

'You don't mean that.'

'He'll never put on the green jersey again, mark my words.'

'You have inside knowledge, Benny?'

'I love seeing the United lads coming in, sicken their arses.'

'You never know,' I say to sicken Benny, 'he could be back yet. We haven't heard the last of this.'

Benny hands me my change of €10, beaming.

'Forget it,' he says, 'he crossed the line and there's no way back.'

All through that week, through the World Cup itself, and through the months that follow, that is the phrase on everybody's lips – an example of how quickly national consensus seals itself into its own pre-prepared, vacuum-packed vocabulary of platitude and mixed metaphor. Reading the papers, you could be forgiven for suspecting that a government leaflet had been delivered door to door, with a glossary of suitable terms to be used in the event of an emergency. P.J. Cunningham, in the *Irish Independent* of 23 May, wrote of 'a demarcation line' between manager and player. James Lawton, in *The Times* of the 24th, even knows the whereabouts of the line: 'now he has crossed a line, at least in the Irish dressing room'. For Paul Hayward, in the *Daily Telegraph* the same morning, it is not so much a question of where as how many: 'You can count the number of times he has crossed the line between trying to cajole less capable and robust colleagues and terrorising them with point-less harangues.' The Ireland midfielder Matt Holland, in the *Independent on Sunday* of the 26th, expressed his belief that 'Keane leapt over the mark in a way that would have done Bob Beamon proud.' Jason McAteer, in the *Sunday Independent* of the same day, said Keane 'was way offside'.

Every discussion I find myself in over the coming weeks ends with that phrase. I go to the supermarket to buy a pound of mince and end up in a screaming match with one of the butcher's assistants. The manager has to step in, but not before the assistant clinches it with a 'crossed the line' parting shot. I turn to find the ladies in the queue behind me are nodding in agreement.

The last straw is a meal in Drogheda on Saturday night, with a couple that are among our oldest pals. Every time we meet up, Liam and I talk footie for a while. Liam knows his parsnips. He is the only other person I know who remembers the World Cup qualifier we played in Paris in 1980, when we fell foul of a couple of dodgy decisions and lost 2–0. I watched it on the telly. He was there. We talk Saipan. Liam is sympathetic and I am trying to seem detached. He has always been a Roy fan. And yet, he can't help concluding that on this occasion Roy 'crossed the line'.

'Liam,' I snap, 'you know as well as I do Roy crossed the fucking line years ago. He crosses it every time he plays for United, every time he plays for Ireland. A week before the World Cup Finals is a hell of a time to pick to clip his wings.'

Before I know it, we are being glanced at from adjacent tables, and my wife is asking me to cool it.

The phrase comes from something Steve Staunton said at the press conference convened twenty minutes (*twenty minutes!*) after the infamous squad meeting in a Chinese restaurant in Saipan: 'There is a line, you can't cross it and unfortunately Roy has crossed it.' It was, I assume, entirely off the cuff. That image, however, has carried enough metaphorical gravity to catch the collective imagination. It places all right-thinking people on the same side of the line as Stan and Niall, peering across at the silenced headbangers and wrongdoers like Roy, and that feels good. None of the assembled hacks bothered to ask Stan on which behavioural models he was basing that conclusion and now it seems not to matter. If that's what Stan said, what Niall Quinn nodded along with, then that's good enough for the nation.

14

Sunday, 26 May. Roy got in early yesterday. Since then he has been 'the disgraced Irish captain walking his golden retriever', pursued by a cavalcade of press and cameramen, white T-shirt and blue jumper knotted around his waist. Yesterday, at teatime, I heard Tommy and Eve chorus at the BBC news, 'What's so defiant about walking a dog?' and fall around laughing. The joke was on me. Danny Baker in *The Times* described the infamous interview as 'an intoxicating joy to read . . . controlled, intelligent, witty and self-effacing conversation'. Is the tide turning? This morning he gets the backing of Sky commentator Andy Gray, and Paul McGrath in the *Sunday Mirror*, Brian Oliver and Tony Adams in the *Observer* and Andy Townsend in the *Sunday Times*. In *Ireland on Sunday* Eamon Dunphy is giving it the man-of-vision speech from the dock treatment: 'Isolated now, he stands more magnificent than ever before, he belongs with the greats of world sport, in the pantheon alongside Ali . . .'

It is also confirmation season, the Catholic Bar Mitzvah. Today half of the extended family converges on Longford for a party for my wife's niece. On the way my wife says, 'Can we drop the subject of Roy Keane? Just for a couple of hours. Please.'

I have been, it's true, a bit of a coiled spring this past forty-eight hours, only ready to snap anywhere or in the face of anyone who shows the merest flicker of dissent. So I understand her nervousness. And yet the indignity of finding myself, at thirty-three, on the receiving end of a pre-emptive ticking-off from my missus needles a little more.

As it transpires, it's no bother. My wife's family are more horse-racing people. All references to Roy are kept to a minimum. The only really vocal person is a cousin-in-law home for a week from St Louis. He reckons Roy is a traitor and says so in a way that suggests he thinks it's what the rest of us want to hear. It clears the sitting room. Everyone crowds round the PC to see if my wife's nephew's band will be UK number one for the second week running. I mope in the background wondering how they can all be so frivolous. After a buffet dinner, there is an hour's chat and then a kickabout that quickly deteriorates into a mudbath. We head for the hills around seven.

On the narrow corkscrew road, outside the townland of Lis-macdermott on the Longford–Westmeath border, we are almost killed. As designated driver I have confined myself to a half-glass of Sauvignon Blanc with the grub and a bucket of coffee. We are descending a long downhill left-hander, praising the countryside's abundance, the whitethorn and cow parsley, when a souped-up sports car comes hurtling towards us on our side of the road. It is all I can do to swerve onto the soft margin, and the sports car skims past us. In the rear-view mirror I catch it hitting the ditch at the top of the hill and bobbling like a Dinky toy back across the road. We sit a few minutes in shock and reverse back up to where the driver is trashing his upside-down car with a golf club.

The natives of the parish sidle out one by one. A woman brings mugs of tea on a tray. Tommy and Eve lean from the window, flagging down cars arriving on the scene. The driver is gradually placated with questions. There was no one else with him. He was at a rally about 20 miles from here, where he had a few cans. He had a row with his brother, and bolted with the brother's car, no insurance and no tax. The solitary local Garda drifts along, unimpressed to have been stirred from his telly. They go over the story one more time and the rest of us stand listening.

'You were at the rally in Baileborough.'

'That's right.'

'You had words with the brother.'

'That's right.'

'And you stormed off.'

'That's right.'

'Touch of the Roy Keanes.'

The way he says it pisses me off. He has given it a rhetorical smirk, and pitched his voice to be audible to the rest of us. We have waited a full half-hour and this is the best he can do.

'I think that's beside the point, Garda.'

'I beg your pardon.'

He is not used to contradiction.

'I don't think this is the time or place to make cheap cracks about Roy Keane.'

We are up and running all over again. Predictably, the officer of the law is against questioning authority in any shape or form. Keane strikes him as an especially insidious instance. A couple of the old boys, loitering on the fringes, chip in. The Garda is right, you don't leave your country in the lurch. I am on the back foot, getting overrun. The Garda actually expresses his belief that Keane has gypsy blood. He then goes on to extemporise on recent rumours about Roy's private life. As he hears it, Mrs Keane has been 'riding the range'. None of us has heard this.

I can see around the side of the moment as well. He we are, a dozen or so standing in the middle of a remote country road. My wife has my jacket around her shoulders, shivering with mild shock, and a mug of sweet, lukewarm tea in her hand. She is peering at all of us at once in disbelief. The car, on its roof on a crushed wire fence, is still smoking. Our kids are fortunate to be merely bored. And yet all we can talk about is Roy and Mick and some island in the Pacific none of us had heard of until a week ago. We are going at it hammer and tongs when a meek dissenting voice in the background brings us to our senses.

'I think he should be allowed back.'

It's the driver of the crashed car. He has a mud graze down the side of his face and he looks a bit flushed. This guy has narrowly missed dismembering me and my family, and now he is my only ally. This is one row I want out of. The Garda says, 'No tax, no insurance, reeking of drink and a car in the ditch . . . I think you'd be well advised to keep your opinions to yourself.'

We make our statements and head off. It is close on midnight when we get in, and almost breakfast time on Monday in Japan.

15

Roy Keane is absolutely gorgeous and now I won't bother watching any of the matches.

Siobhra, Dublin. www.ireland.com

Roy has become an unlikely pin-up. Traditionally, that role fell to the likes of Jason McAteer or Phil Babb. But in recent years Jason's hairline, once the centre of a 'Head and Shoulders' commercial, has gone into recession. Roy has given the pints a miss, shed a stone and aged into his looks. Towards the end of the qualifying campaign even our own mother, to the mortification of her grown-up sons, was known to interrupt the solemnity of the national anthem to call our skipper 'a hell of a fine thing'. In November 2001, after we had qualified, the first issue of the magazine *Gay Ireland* named him as an icon. Morrissey, ex-lead singer of The Smiths, has his own camp homage called 'Roy's Keen' in the solo CD *Maladjusted*.

If he apologises, should he be given one more chance? In the past week ladies, perhaps more used to asking themselves that question, have been tripping each other up to say in print how attractive they suddenly find him. Roisin Ingle, columnist with the *Irish Times* Magazine, confesses to a crush. After a brief encounter at Dublin Airport, she writes:

That was it. I spent the next couple of hours watching Keano watch everyone else and totally reviewing my no bad boys policy. I know I'm not the only one who felt it . . . there were intense discussions in the office about his allure.

Siobhan Cronin, in the *Irish Independent* Review, asks where 'Ireland's greatest sex symbol' has been hiding:

> But if those Eastern clouds that swept in last week had any silver lining, it was the emergence of the greatest boost to the Irish thirty-something female psyche since TV3 started screening *Sex and the City* . . . Talk of his battles with 'inner demons' and depression and being left out in the cold by his team mates makes him all the more attractive.

Cronin also sees 'a chink of light for us hopefuls' in the interview with Paul Kimmage in today's *Sunday Independent*. A quote is published as a headline on the front page. It reads: 'I said "They'll always be my kids, but you won't necessarily always be my wife." ' The words, however, were spoken in response to a question about his kids' names tattooed on his upper right arm and, within the context of the interview, clearly meant as a joke.

The quote, and manner in which it was reprinted, was obviously designed to feed into the oodles of rumours about Roy's love life, none of which has been substantiated. According to one report, the rumours began on a website dedicated exclusively to World Cup gossip. The site predicted that the *News of the World* would publish an exposé of Roy's misdemeanours. Later in the week, however, the editor of the *News of the World* called Michael Kennedy, Roy's solicitor and agent, to disassociate her paper from those reports. Last Friday, Theresa Keane received two separate phone calls from the same woman who claimed to be her husband's pregnant mistress. During the second of those calls, Theresa threatened to bring the law in if the calls continued. They didn't.

The rumours are still out there, thanks to people like that Lismacdermott Garda. That he has been having an affair. That he has gone and left a sixteen year old in the family way. That it is his wife who has been engaged in extra-curricular activities and

God help the cad when Roy gets his hands on him. 'I'm supposedly sleeping with more women than I could dream of,' Roy will later remark. 'I've got dozens of women pregnant, apparently in Dublin of all places.' Up until the phrase 'Roy's love life' was coined, and notwithstanding the procreation of a quartet of mini Keanes, it never occurred to any of us that he had one.

16

Tommy (*seated on the coffee table*): 'Is this now?'

Me (*upright and speechless, having just been called in from the kitchen in apron and washing-up gloves, a Brillo pad in my right hand*): 'Shhh.'

Roy (*tanned, in grey sweatshirt with white crew neck, in some studio*): 'On Thursday evening the storm clouds were brewing. I was told there was a meeting at 7.30.'

Tommy: 'Was this last year?'

Me: 'Shhh.'

Roy: 'He had a piece of paper in his hand and I knew it was about the interview. I stayed calm. I knew he was going to make a point.'

Tommy: 'Is this now?'

My Wife: 'Shush Tom, please.'

Roy: 'I knew we were moving to a different training place. I was talking to all the players.'

Eve: 'He looks yellow.'

Me (*petulantly*): 'Please!'

Roy: 'People say I probably shouldn't have reacted the way I did. Of course, hindsight is a great thing. I think I was forced into a corner. I really was. That's my honest belief. There was only one way I was going to come out and that was fighting.'

Eve: 'This is boring.'

Me: 'Out.'

Roy: 'I expect them to stick together. I am well aware of that. It's a squad and they all back Mick.'

Tommy: 'Is he back out there?'

Me: 'Shush.'

Roy: 'The family are glad to see me.'

Tommy: 'Is he back in Japan?'

Me: 'For the last time, no.'

Roy: 'I just can't wait to take her out to dinner, and I won't be wearing dark glasses.'

Tommy (*lip wobbling*): 'That was the first time, actually.'

Me: 'Please . . .'

Roy: 'Dead right it hurts.'

Eve: 'He's a cry-baby.'

Me: 'Out!'

Roy: 'I can't see it happening. We'll have to see. I really don't know. I'd love to play in the World Cup, but I have to stand up for what I believe in.'

Tommy: 'Is he going back?'

Me: 'Don't know.'

Roy: 'The match is on Saturday. We're running out of time. Maybe there is a way. Who knows? We'll have to wait and see.'

Tommy: 'Is he going back to Japan?'

Me: 'Maybe. Maybe.'

It catches the whole country off guard. I am on my knees with my head in the oven, cleaning, when my son starts flapping and shouting excitedly. It is broadcast before the nine o'clock news and overruns. The pubs of the nation are dumbstruck. In Saipan, because of the absence of a satellite link, all the Irish journalists cram into one hotel room to listen to it being relayed down the phone from someone's wife back at home. At the end of the year it will appear second in the annual TV ratings. Almost one million open mouths. Cameroon, Germany and Saudi Arabia won't come close. Spain alone will pip it by a hair's breadth.

Tommy Gorman, RTÉ's Belfast correspondent, is covering the saga only because the usual London correspondent is on leave. He has been in contact with Michael Kennedy since last Friday. Kennedy said that they were already in discussion with Martin Bashir and ITV who were offering £100,000. Gorman talked up the wisdom of the Irish route and Kennedy promised to call back. Gorman travelled to Manchester and hung around outside Roy's house. From time to time he glimpsed the kids gazing out onto the sea of camera crews from one of the upstairs windows. Kennedy's number flashed up on Gorman's mobile shortly after 10.30 this morning. White smoke. The ballroom was booked in Manchester's Moat House Hotel. When they were through, Roy told Gorman that he went into the interview determined he wasn't going back and found himself being swayed. 'You made me change my mind,' he said. He also said to use every second of it and left to collect his kids from school. He dropped Kennedy back at the airport and, saying goodbye, agreed to make no decisions, to wait and see.

'I didn't hear anything resembling an apology. Wasn't that the point?'

My wife, noticing how buoyant I am tonight, is attempting to smooth the road to disappointment. I pass no remarks. She doesn't understand, I tell myself.

17

Sir, As an NUI graduate, I am not at all impressed by the idea of giving a doctorate to Roy Keane. Who gave the university a mandate to give this award? I do not agree with giving these awards to players who are obscenely over-paid, who desert this country to earn obscene amounts, who have bad disciplinary records and who excel merely at kicking a ball around a field under a foreign code. What is the university playing at? Where is its social conscience? What are the standards and models? Yours etc,

Alan Cooney,

Castleknock,

Dublin 15

Irish Independent, 16 May 2002

Sir, I have to say I am far from impressed by the recent title awarded Dr Roy Keane. Surely An Taoiseach [The Prime Minister] would have been far more appropriate? Yours etc,

Ronan Kearney,

Dundrum,

Dublin 16

Irish Independent, 22 May 2002

The real Taoiseach found himself in the thick of Ireland's World Cup mayhem. Bertie Ahern had always been cute enough to use football in much the same way that Tony Blair has cultivated his love of Chelsea. It is his direct line to the common man, and one that you suspect will never be cut off. The Taoiseach's passion for Man United has been unapologetically on the record for many years. Once, he even appeared as an expert panellist on the RTÉ edition of *The Premiership*. His ratings in the popularity polls had not slumped, nor were there local or European elections in the offing. Sure, it was a PR stunt. But behind that stunt lay an image of Bertie chewing the fat over footie like you or me.

Even before the whole Roy/Mick civil war blew up, there were a couple of other minor shadows over Bertie's enjoyment of the World Cup. Firstly, there was the business of a general election. Since last Christmas there had been considerable speculation as to how the Korea/Japan feel-good factor could be surfed to make the outgoing Taoiseach incoming. The choice of 17 May as the date when the country would go to the polls was also the morning after our sayonara to the Boys in Green against Nigeria, and the day on which they flew east.

Secondly, there is the more opaque business of Ireland's joint bid with Scotland to host the Euro 2008 finals. Central to that bid are two Dublin stadiums, one virtual and one actual. The former will only ever exist in populist nomenclature as 'The Bertie Bowl'. This is the Taoiseach's pet project, his dream of building a 60,000-seater, state-of-the-art sports arena on the city's green belt, primarily as a base for the national soccer team. The latter is Croke Park, home of the Gaelic Athletic Association and Bertie's beloved Dublin Gaelic football team. Croker has recently been renovated with the help of promised public funds to the tune of €76million. It is now an 80,000-seater, state-of-the-art sports arena on the edge of the city centre, in the heart of Bertie's constituency. It has been named in the Euro 2008 bid, and the UEFA delegation will stroll its pastures, despite the caveat that soccer has never been played there.

Traditionalists argue that the ban is not on 'foreign sports' as such, but that only national teams representing a 32-county Ireland are acceptable. If it were that simple then the Irish rugby team, which selects players from North as well as South, would surely have togged out in Croker long ago. The conundrum is that for the Euro 2008 bid to get off the ground, the GAA had to lift the ban on soccer being played in its spiritual home – fast. Despite the vast majority of its own players' association being in favour of opening the doors to soccer, there is little hope of that happening in the near future.

The Taoiseach happened to be canvassing in Cork on 10 May, the same day Roy received his honorary doctorate. Bertie hung around much longer than he usually would, kissing extra babies and pacing with hands in pockets, hoping in vain for a photo opportunity. By pure coincidence, Bertie was also in the airport at lunchtime on Friday, 17 May. The squad had queued with the hoi polloi to check in, had signed autographs and smiled into the cameras of travelling and non-travelling fans, and were then corralled into the Skyview Lounge for a sponsors' reception. It was at that point that Bertie appeared, with a retinue of camera crews, shaking hands and slapping backs. After much jostling, the captain was backed into a corner with which he clearly wasn't happy and much was made of the fact the he didn't stand:

The Bertie thing. I've met Bertie before. I think there was an election that day, was there? . . . Don't get me wrong but there are always hidden agendas, always, always, hidden agendas. Bertie is a bloody nice bloke. I've met him a few times, he's a big United fan, I know all that but it's just . . . it should have been better organised.

Bertie was on his holidays, resting on the laurels of an election landslide, the Thursday when the bad news broke. Several reports had the Department of the Taoiseach inundated with telephone calls urging some sort of political intervention. Among the callers were representatives of the Irish Football Supporters' Association, whose disarmingly direct solution involved the Taoiseach jumping on a plane to Saipan immediately, and generally knocking Roy's and Mick's heads together. Bertie, perhaps horrified at the prospect of seventeen hours in the government jet, suggested there was little he could do when neither manager nor player seemed interested in a reconciliation. However, he left on the table the offer of his services as a broker, should they be required. His office waited until late on Thursday evening before issuing an official statement:

I share the disappointment of all Irish fans that Roy will not be participating in the World Cup in Japan. It is very unfortunate that events, which are not fully clear at this time, have conspired to deprive the Irish team of his great talent.

Despite the official version that had the Taoiseach being appalled by the 'English c★★t' reports, Bertie was working away in the background. On Thursday night he rang Brendan Menton, the General Secretary of the FAI. It was then early on Friday morning in Saipan and Menton had only just arrived from Ireland. Bertie asked Menton to ask Mick if he could have a word an hour and a half before the squad was due to fly off. Roy, behind the closed door of his single room, could hear his team-mates in the corridor. Mick was finishing packing when Menton knocked. Mick said there would be no point. He had made his decision and there was no going back. When Menton called Bertie ten minutes later, Bertie said he understood.

Precisely whom the Taoiseach spoke to over last weekend is still unclear. If you swallowed every rumour at face value then Bertie conversed with Alex Ferguson, Niall Quinn, the president of FIFA Sepp Blatter, and even Bono. Apart from his altogether genuine love of football and the Irish team, you couldn't help but feel that Bertie had spotted what press secretaries term 'a unique opportunity'. Even with the election feather in his cap Bertie recognised that credit for Roy on the park in Niigata next Saturday could be his biggest political coup. Speaking on the steps of Government Buildings, shortly before the interview with Tommy Gorman is due to be broadcast on national TV, Bertie admits to losing his beauty sleep:

> There is a huge, huge public interest in this . . . There is no doubt that there is a passionate feeling by people in this country that if this could be reconciled in some way, everyone would not alone be happier but would sleep happier.

The Taoiseach then stumbles into the eye of the storm the same night. Having watched the interview in full, he drops in to pay his respects at a party to mark the retirement of one of his constituents. He experiences at first hand the extremity of emotions around the story, which he later describes as 'quite amazing'. Most of the party-goers have watched the interview on the big screen. When the Taoiseach puts his head around the door, the debate has become so intense that many of the OAPs seem on the brink of throwing punches. Bertie can handle it no more, and makes his apologies. 'There weren't too many people under sixty at it,' he later remarks. 'It almost came to blows. I got out.'

18

Mid-morning, 28 May. I have the house to myself. The airwaves are awash with reactions to last night's interview, fretting over the absence of the 'S' word. I surf the web and immediately the swelling bubble of optimism pops. The BBC Sport home page leads this morning with the headline 'Irish Players Back McCarthy'. The squad has drafted its own press statement and it was issued in what must have been the wee hours of Greenwich Mean Time. Having heard what Roy has had to say and not to say, they reckon it's in everyone's interest if he walks his dog for the next few weeks.

Regrettably, the manner of Roy's behaviour prior to his departure from Saipan, and the comments attributed to him since, have left the staff and players in no doubt that the best interests of the squad are best served without Roy's presence.

After going to such lengths to underline his authority, McCarthy seems to have abdicated power of squad selection to a smattering of senior players. I start shouting and banging doors at the same time. I tumble the whites from the washing machine and stomp into the back garden. I am still muttering 'Stupid bastards' when I catch the eye of our neighbour across the fence.

In the afternoon, I collect the kids at the pool again. While Eve is drying her wet hair in our bedroom, Tommy and me go into the box room to try the web one last time. The to-ing and fro-ing has lost him. He knows Roy was sent home. He saw the interview last night, and has heard the talk about Roy returning. The rest is above his head. I don't think he will fully understand until the team sheet is read out on Saturday morning.

We go into email first. One comes in from a friend called Paul who we used know in Dublin, but who these days works in a film distribution company in the heart of Manhattan. My wife was over there in March and brought their six-month-old son an Ireland jersey with the Korea/Japan 2002 logo. Among other news, Paul says:

Utter anguish in our house over the Keano saga. Horrible stuff, and I've been very much in Roy's camp since the beginning, but am beginning to waver a little now.

Still online, we click the net icon and hold our crossed fingers up to each other. It works. Our search engine's home page is leading with a recent bulletin. Niall has given a distraught press conference since the release of the statement. He has said that the younger players were campaigning to get Roy flown back. The statement was written after Mick left them with an ultimatum, but wasn't supposed to be released so soon. The report also claims that sources close to Michael Kennedy say he is currently in the process of drafting an apology acceptable to both parties. And most incredible of all, there is rumoured to be a private jet on standby.

'Oh fuck!'

'Dad!'

I email Paul with the news:

Hold on to your hats! Newsflash just in to say a plane is waiting at Manchester Airport. Seems Big Niall gave a tearful press conference this afternoon to say the players want him back. Roy's agent has now admitted that they are wording an apology as I write. Justice!

We wait online a couple of minutes, and an immediate reply from a US server comes ping-ponging back across the Atlantic:

IS IT TRUE, CONOR? IS IT TRUE?

I hold on until five and call my younger brother. He is just in from work, knackered. It takes a couple of retellings for his voice to change register. He has spent all day in a workshop, deafened by the whirr of machines slicing timber and the radio at full blast on some pop channel. This is clearly news to him and he doubts its authenticity. I leave him to check the text on the TV. He calls back within a minute. He doesn't sound so tired any more.

19

The Republic of Ireland was the only team granted a Papal audience during Italia 1990. The visit was set up by Monsignor Liam Boyle, a native of Newcastle West and self-appointed padre to the players. Fr Liam attends all home games and most away, saying a squad mass the day before every one. The only perennials are Niall Quinn and Steven Staunton. Fr Liam also prays during games, especially when the team is up against it. 'I remember praying a lot during the last Holland game,' he told the *Irish Daily Mirror*. Now he is preparing for a showdown with the witch doctors Cameroon have been reported to use: 'I've heard Cameroon used superstition during the recent African Cup. I'm prepared for that. I can bless the team at any time and I'd have no problem doing it.'

On the same day as the feature on Fr Liam, the *Mirror* also gave a website address – www.catholicireland.net – that includes dates and times of masses in Japan offered specifically for the success of the Ireland team. For those of us lucky enough not to be travelling there was our very own 'Cut-Out-&-Keep-It World Cup Prayer', to be said by the whole family 'prior to kick-off and in the event of extra time':

> Dear Lord you gave us football to enjoy healthy and friendly rivalry
> Take care of our Irish team as they journey to Japan and Korea
> May they represent their country with pride and distinction
> Help them to play to the best of their God-given abilities
> Let our team be supported by our prayers for their success
> St Patrick, patron of Ireland, watch over our team, protect them from injury, keep their spirits high, their eyes keen and their feet swift
> Give them the strength to tackle every challenge as they journey towards their goal
> Let them return to our country safely, with honour
> And if it be pleasing to you, God, with the World Cup. Amen.

Roy's arrival for World Cup duty at the Holiday Inn on the evening of Wednesday the 15th was treated by at least one of his colleagues as a second coming. He had missed the photo shoot with the President, Mary McAleece, been whisked across a packed foyer to get fitted into his official blazer and then joined the lads in the dining area just as they were tucking in. 'I don't expect we'll see him before the first of June,' Jason McAteer had told one reporter. Suddenly there he was, official kit on and mess tray in hand. In his diary column for the *Sunday Independent* of

19 May, McAteer records the tongue-in-cheek relief with which he greeted the appearance of their messiah:

I was overcome by a sudden urge I should have controlled. Maybe it was a reaction to what had been written. Maybe, deep down, I was genuinely relieved to see him. I jumped up instinctively, bowed in homage and shouted 'HALLELUJAH'.

If Roy was the plain old saviour then Niall Quinn, thanks to his highly publicised night for kids' charities, had recently been canonised as the patron saint of Irish football. To many he has become, affectionately, 'Saint Niall'. This seems to have become a source of silent hilarity for Roy, whose earliest advertising campaign for Diadora boots featured his eyes tinted red and the by-line: 'We've sold our souls to the devil.' Also, his own covert charitable work had become the stuff of urban myth in which Roy gets lit as the Robin Hood of Irish football. Jason McAteer, in the same piece, presented the most categorical confirmation of its truth:

It has long been a tradition on the day before games in Dublin for the players to slip into Grafton Street for a bit of shopping. Roy never shops but often slips out the side door of the hotel to visit sick kids in hospitals. I know this to be true because I was asked to join him once but refused because it really upsets me to see children suffer.

Out of disgust at the absence of secrecy and the credit his team-mate had been given for one charitable splurge, Roy christened Niall 'Mother Teresa'. It stuck. To those of us who took Roy's side, Niall became 'The Mother Teresa of Irish Football'. It had a delicious boldness Roy wouldn't let go. In the lift of the Saipan Hyatt with Tom Humphries last Wednesday, on the way down from the third floor after their infamous interview, he asked how ghosting Niall's autobiography was coming along. Tom said it was fine. Roy smiled and looked at his feet and couldn't stop himself asking, 'Will you get most of it done from home, or will you have to go to Calcutta?'

'I'm sure the man upstairs is guiding me along the way,' Roy had also said less flippantly towards the end of the same interview, 'putting a few obstacles in my way.' We may never know what Dr John Buckley, the Catholic Bishop of Cork and Ross, made of this interpretation of divine intervention as a sort of spiritual heat of *It's a Knockout*. But we do know that Bishop Buckley, popularly nicknamed 'The Bowling Bishop', spoke on several RTÉ radio programmes appealing for a last-minute 'softening of hearts on both sides'. Bishop Buckley's closeness to the Keane inner circle is underlined by the fact that he is even privy to Roy's home number. Around three o'clock on 28 May, shortly after his appeal on air, Roy is out collecting the girls from school when he calls. The Bishop leaves a message on the voicemail and waits. Eventually he leaves, already late for an appointment. It is one of many near misses that litter the story's margins. When Roy returns the call twenty minutes later, the housekeeper answers. He asks her to tell the Bishop he rang, and she writes his name on diocesan headed paper beside the phone.

By that stage the Irish squad, minus Roy, was enjoying the hospitality of the farming town of Izumo just outside Tokyo. After their application to be an official World Cup host city was knocked back, the Mayor of Izumo started making overtures to Ireland even before we had qualified. Invocations were made regularly at the city's shrines and to its fifty million Shinto gods. Mayor Nishio says that invocations became especially intense, and that he himself prayed at the famous Tachai temple, around the time of our home tie with Holland last September.

The General Secretary of the FAI, Brendan Menton, whiles away the morning and afternoon of Tuesday, the 28th, shrine-hopping on his own. He has continued to pull transcontinental strings to get

Roy back, in spite of the players' statement issued earlier that day saying baldly that they backed the captain's expulsion. He is seen to light candles and make donations and pause in moments of proverbial 'silent prayer'. Such is Menton's information from Roy's advisors, and such is the strength of his belief that night that the player will apologise, he tells Mick to expect a call from Cheshire some time after dawn. He turns in, he will later tell journalists, 80 per cent certain that it will happen. Then, around 3am local time, the phone on the bedside locker wakes him.

20

Late afternoon, 28 May. My wife heard the headlines on the car radio, sitting in the tailback on the bypass. The newscaster said that a statement was expected very soon from Roy's solicitor, then cut away to speculation about the formation of the incoming cabinet. Shortly after, my wife's brother lands. He works in town for about three two-week periods in every year and stays with us when he has an early start. He belongs resolutely to the Regulars rowing in behind the manager. He has been full of the joys since last Thursday. I have the good grace to allow him to get his blazer off and settle with a mug of tea.

'Oh by the way . . .' I say, facing in towards the worktop, unable to stifle a smile.

'Yes?'

'Looks like the main man is poised to re-enter the fray.'

'Who?'

I smile again.

'Keane?'

I start laughing.

'Bullshit.'

''fraid not.'

It is one of those not-remotely-rare moments when the biggest pleasure of your day involves posting a black cloud on someone else's. I am doing my utmost not to gloat, and clearly I am not making a great fist of it.

'He's going to apologise?'

'Let's just say his solicitor is wording *an apology*. I suspect it'll be a bit like Dev's "empty formula".'

This hurts. My wife's brother is a diehard anti-Republican. Between the wars, members of the Irish parliament were still obliged to take an oath of allegiance to the Crown. The 'empty formula' was devised as a means of getting around the oath by mumbling it sarcastically, without meaning or feeling.

'Bullshit.'

'Maybe you should ring RTÉ, since they seem to have the wrong story altogether.'

He looks at my wife for verification, and she yields a so-they-say shrug. He knows it's true, or at least he knows we think it's true. He seems genuinely wounded, and prepared to clutch at straws.

'They'll never get him out in time.'

'You'd think not all right . . .'

I have saved this detail for the knockout punch. Although fractionally below the belt, it does the trick.

'. . . but JP McManus has offered his private jet.'

JP McManus, professional punter and racehorse owner, is one of Ireland's wealthiest men. My wife's brother is a great man for the gee-gees. He is having difficulty coming to terms with the idea of someone he has admired from afar, someone he always assumed to be one of them, batting for the opposition.

'Bullshit.'

'If you insist. I must say, I thought it very decent of JP. I suppose one VIP recognises another.'

'*VIP*! He's a little gurrier who doesn't deserve such kindness.'

The only blight on the moment is the manner in which my wife's brother takes it. He takes it very well, much better than I would if the situation was reversed. After a week of heartache, I am playing the smug prick to a T. If I were him, I would have decked me a long time ago. Perhaps that's part of the difference, the reason we have taken the sides we have taken. He finishes his tea and graciously offers to take the kids to McDonald's.

The phone doesn't ring. There is no advance on the last dispatch on the web. Will we ever find out what the phone conversation between Mick and himself is like? Perhaps it has already happened, and Roy is packing his bags for a second time. If he is, then it is probably with an even heavier heart. Not only is there the prospect of the isolation and boredom and homesickness he factors into international duty. There will also be the awkwardness of meeting his team-mates again, most for the first time since storming from the restaurant in Saipan; of knowing he has been the butt of most of their running jokes in the interim; of trying not to bear grudges for those who put their delight at his banishment on record; of having rooms hush the moment he steps into them; of not meeting the manager's eye once in three weeks; of trying to prove on the pitch that he was worth the fuss.

21

Someone laid a wreath at the door of FAI headquarters in Merrion Square in Dublin last Friday morning. It has lain there all weekend. It was pictured front page of the *Irish Times* the next day: a bunch of lilies, with a handwritten commiseration card that reads 'Irish Football 1/6/1921–23/5/2002'. The first date refers approximately to the establishment of the FAI, the second date is last Thursday. A vigil by disgruntled fans has been swelling in Merrion Square, and uniformed Gardaí have been on duty all weekend.

Dundalk has been at the forefront of the protests. Last Thursday night a handful of desperados got together in a pub and instigated the 'Bring Roy Back 2 Japan' petition. The main mover of the group was the hearse driver for a local funeral director. They decommissioned one of the company's superannuated vehicles, a 1979 Merc, painted it the colours of the flag, christened it the official 'Bring Roy Back Limo' and attached number plates to that effect. They left from Earl Street at lunchtime.

Several times during the afternoon they had live link-ups with the local radio station, LMFM. The bloke in the passenger seat did the talking. His name is Keith Duffy. Before they hit the village of Slane, halfway to the capital on the old road, the story had been picked up by all the national stations. The Merc is so old that it has no in-built radio, so they had to tune in on a battery-powered ghettoblaster on the back seat. It became apparent that the story was getting coverage only because the radio people believed their Keith Duffy was *the* Keith Duffy. It was too good to pass up, a Boyzone ex-member and present *Coronation Street* star campaigning for clemency for the disgraced Irish captain. So their Keith gave his best Dublin accent a stab, said it was more than his job's worth to give away forthcoming plotlines and by the time they hit the northern edge of the city there were well-wishers waving from their doorways.

At Glasnevin Cemetery, resting place of Charles Stewart Parnell among others, a squad car was hovering on the hard shoulder. The lads thought they were being summonsed for the racket. They were, in fact, being accorded a Garda escort through the city centre. They got cheered and heckled down O'Connell Street. As many people declined as accepted to sign the petition. When the 'Bring Roy Back Limo' finally parked on Merrion Square they had 1,200 names and the press corps was expecting them. The *Star*, that has all week run its own 'Bring Roy Back' campaign, gave them a half-page photo and a headline that read 'What A Car-azy Bid'. In the

Daily Mirror they got less space but pride of place beneath the editor's 'Comment'. The small piece claimed that 'FAI bosses were yesterday handed a petition by a group of diehard supporters.' Not strictly true. I got speaking to one of the boys' mothers and she said they rang the bell of FAI headquarters all right, but there was no answer.

The best picture in the weekend papers is of a lone protestor sitting on the wall of his back yard, beside a sign. He is Stephen Treston, a taxi driver from Donaghmede. His sign, for the eyes of passers-by, reads on three lines: SACK MCCARTHY AND FAI FAT CATS KEEP ROY KEANE. The sign is obviously handmade, black and white and there is a comma after every word on the first two lines. Stephen is beside it in an Ireland tracksuit. His arms are crossed and his eyes are gazing towards some horizon beyond the camera, possibly Saipan. 'Nobody is really bothered any more,' he complains. 'Some people are not going to watch the matches because he is not playing.'

Last Friday, the tradesmen of a west of Ireland building site downed tools and picketed in protest. The workers on The Station House in Clifden, County Galway, were calling for a national strike until Roy is reinstated. A spokesman for the Construction Federation of Ireland described their actions as 'outrageous, irresponsible and reckless'. The bookmaker Paddy Power has since organised an email petition asking Mick McCarthy to accept Roy back into the squad if Roy apologises. By close of business on Tuesday over 10,000 names have clicked on. At that stage, there are estimated to be 400 protestors chanting outside the association's HQ on Merrion Square. A plasterer from Dublin pledges €100,000 of his life savings to a charity of Roy's choice if he agrees to return. One thirty-year-old woman is arrested after she pelts its doors and windows with eggs. At the same time there is a 'Reinstate Roy' march through the streets of Cork city. The protestors leave Bishop Lucey Park at 5pm, press-gang up Patrick Street and return to the park about 1,500 strong, singing 'All we are saying is give Roy a chance'. Around half past six a cab driver who has his radio on yells, 'There's a statement, there's a statement' and the singing falls silent.

22

Early evening, 28 May. The doorbell goes. Tommy always wins the race and rings even though someone invariably is coming with a key behind him. The others are still getting out of the car.

'Roy's not going back.'

He has a big flushed face, a small Coke in one hand and a Happy Meal toy in the other.

'How do you know?'

'It was on the news in the car.'

'Serious?'

'Serious.'

Tommy's uncle is not far behind, duly taking his turn to crow and watch me squirm.

'Well I'm delighted,' he roars. 'He's a knacker and he should never have been let out there in the first place.'

'It's very sad,' is all I can muster. 'Very, very sad.'

'Sad, my granny. It's the best news in a week. Now we can get on with the real business of the World Cup without having to pander to that spoilt brat.'

'He got them there.'

I say it softly, matter-of-factly, not shouting.

'Oh he got them there, did he? All on his ownio!'

'Pretty much.'

'Football's an eleven-man game, and well you know it.'

I turn on the machine upstairs and send a last email to Paul. I figure he hasn't heard the latest. I figure he is sitting in his office in

60

New York at a few minutes past three in the afternoon, going through the motions and still clinging to the myth of a private jet purring on a runway in Manchester. Is it true? I hit Reply, write:

No, it seems it isn't nor ever was. oh God . . .

There is no getting away from it. The news has started early, sifting through the major events of the past week. There are pundits in the studio, ex-players on the line from England, giving their opinions. They all expected an apology, a comeback. Now that it hasn't happened, they are urging us to look forward and forget Roy. We are shown footage of the protestors outside the FAI headquarters in Dublin, at the moment when the news was broken. There are a few tears and a wide-angle shot of the crowd dispersing away into the city.

My wife's brother has gone out for a bite to eat. Up until then, Tommy sat in the kitchen drawing an Ireland strip with the gel pens he got for his birthday, and doing a lot of huffing. Now that his uncle is off radar, he sits up on my knee and cries his heart out. It reminds me of the morning of his first day at school. He is still that small boy learning how to play it tough, that there are things from which his parents can't protect him.

'I thought he was supposed to say sorry.'

'It's okay.'

'He was supposed to say sorry.'

23

In the last twenty-four hours spent in Saipan, there was some uncertainty about Roy's travel arrangements home. FAI treasurer John Delaney admitted to not having the foggiest about how the ex-captain was getting back. 'It's out of my hands,' the association's travel agent said. At the time there had been the fanciful suggestion that United sent a private jet.

The irony is that Roy's first run-in with Irish officialdom, and frequently cited as the foundation of antipathy between himself and McCarthy, involved keeping the squad waiting on the bus to take them to Logan Airport for their evening flight home. It was the last day of a US tour, 1992. McCarthy, as captain and senior player, had tried to give him a dressing-down and received 'one of those sarky comments of his'. Since then, Roy has grown to associate the difference in attitude to flight between club and country with a difference in ambition. In 1999, for example, United flew to Barcelona for their Champions' League final by Concorde. It was Ferguson's way of reminding his players, by implication, of the standard expected of them and to which they should aspire. On the flight home, the non-playing captain sat alone at the back while the champagne flowed.

Flight became the first bone of contention during the qualifying campaign for Korea/Japan. In March 2001, between away wins against Cyprus and Andorra in a four-day period, Roy gave an interview to Paul Kimmage in the *Sunday Independent* in which he complained bitterly about the flying arrangements of the FAI. The staff and officials and Mick McCarthy flew first class to away matches, while the players sat cramped in economy. He said it was the kind of thing that made him contemplate retiring from the international game. Initially, there was widespread disbelief. Could this be true? In response, the then General Secretary of the association, Bernard O'Byrne, said he would happily swim to Cyprus if it helped the team's cause and kept Roy playing.

The captain's words had an impact, temporarily. The team found itself upgraded to the front rows on the Barcelona–Dublin leg of its itinerary. The blazers had to swallow their pride and squeeze through to steerage. Roy was one of the last on board. His team-mates burst spontaneously into applause, to which he permitted himself the frivolity of a solitary theatrical bow. Most of the players, unused to the trappings of the Premier League élite and the glamour of European competition, couldn't believe their luck: the space, the upholstery, the individual TV screens, the freshly squeezed juice. They called it 'Roy Class'. From then until the end of the qualifying campaign the team flew 'Roy Class'.

Then there was the flight to Saipan, or *flights*. As they were waiting in Departures in Dublin, one of two leprechauns promoting the *Sun* threw his arm around Roy and roared, 'C'mon Keano, cheer up.' Roy availed of the stopover at Schipol to berate two journalists who had criticised his non-appearance at Niall's testimonial as a snub. There was one rumour, which we all believed and repeated flippantly at the time even though we had no proof. So certain were Holland of their progress to Korea/Japan that a charter had already been booked and paid for with KLM. 'It's said,' Niall will write, 'that when we knocked Holland out of the World Cup qualifying stages, the FAI did a deal with the Dutch FA and bought their flight tickets off them.' The Amsterdam–Tokyo leg, when they finally boarded, took seventeen hours. Roy sat alone in knee-length socks to ward off DVT and watched DVDs. In Tokyo the squad was finally corralled away from drunk fans into an executive lounge. By the time they reached Saipan they had been twenty-three hours in the air

The day after the showdown, going their separate ways, the squad's flight to Izumo left early and Roy had to wait until six in the evening. The Izumo charter was covered by the mayor of that city in return for the Irish team agreeing to use Izumo as their Japanese base. FAI officials and staff claimed the business-class seats before the team arrived and the players moaned about being downgraded so soon from 'Roy Class'.

Tommy still believes Roy glimpsed the snowcaps of Tajikistan in darkness. We know now that United did not send a jet as we all believed. They booked his flights, picking a route that would seem unlikely to the paparazzi: Saipan–Guam, Guam–Hong Kong, Hong Kong–London, London–Manchester. Four other tickets out of Saipan are believed to have been booked in his name, to throw over-zealous reporters off the scent. One journalist admits he knew he had been conned when, after a lengthy delay at the departure gate for Tokyo, a stewardess came down and asked if his friend 'Passenger Keane' would be boarding soon. Passenger Keane was already in the air. He got delayed several hours in Guam and an English guy, seeing he was cut up, made him a mug of tea. He was met by a BA buggy in Hong Kong and sat awake first class most of the way. He was ushered into BA hospitality in Heathrow, where Michael Kennedy was waiting. United had sent a car to meet them in Manchester. There were hundreds of reporters and cameramen camped outside his house.

The final flight is the one that didn't happen: Manchester–Tokyo, four days before Ireland's opening match with Cameroon in Niigata. So many rumours were hurtling around at the time that most have since been disproved. We know that the FAI, certain that a conciliatory long-distance call would be made in the no-man's-land between Tuesday the 28th and Wednesday the 29th, had booked and paid for a ticket back to Japan in Keane's name. We know also that Michael Kennedy was offered the wings of several separate parties: the Manchester United club jet; the private jet of the Government of Ireland; those of business tycoons Sir Anthony O'Reilly, JP McManus, Dermot Desmond and Eddie Jordan; and a fourteen-seater reportedly chartered by the radio station 98FM at a cost of €177,660. For a whole extraordinary afternoon the nation really believed that one of those offers had been accepted, that it sat fuelled and waiting for clearance on the tarmac at one of the smaller gates of Manchester Airport. Whose jet was it? And was that true? We shall probably never know for sure.

24

While I appreciate all the support I have received and all the
efforts which have been made by a number of people on behalf
of all parties involved in this unfortunate matter, I do not
consider that the best interests of Irish football will be served
by my returning to the World Cup.

Roy Keane, 28 May 2002

That it ended with contradictions and more FAI cock-ups should
be hilarious. I read the papers and weep into my Weetabix, the
morning of Wednesday the 29th.

Niall Quinn spilled all beans worth spilling at what seems to have
been a pretty hot and heavy session with the media at 5pm (his time)
yesterday. He said that he was approached last Saturday by one of
the younger squad members claiming to represent a pro-Roy
faction. Niall and Michael Kennedy chipped away over the weekend, to the point that by Monday evening (our time) both believed
a reconciliation more probable than possible, and Niall and Staunton sat up all Monday night for word of the TV interview. He called
his wife, Gillian.

'I got a bit ratty with her because it was unclear what had been
said.'

The press boys assembled outside the Izumo Royal at around
6.45am. Brendan McKenna, the FAI press officer, was woken by
hotel staff and, bleary eyed before the waiting cameras, confessed he
hadn't the foggiest about any interview. Then McCarthy an hour
later, impromptu in thickening sunlight on the hotel steps, 'The call
has got to come.' Which the squad interpreted as an olive branch.
For the next three hours word circulated around their corridor that

the captain was already in the air. But McCarthy hadn't heard or read the interview. When he did, again on computer printout, he called another team meeting for 10.30am. What he said in the first twenty minutes of that meeting, Niall says, 'effectively ended any chance of Roy Keane appearing at the World Cup'. He told the lads to have a chat among themselves. Their statement was drafted in the back of the bus to training. It was agreed, however, that the statement be withheld until after a press conference with McCarthy and Brendan Menton later that day, so Niall felt they still had time.

When Niall came off the training ground a couple of hours later he discovered, to his horror, that the other Brendan – McKenna – had released the statement during his own daily briefing with the media. In fairness to McKenna, he was left alone to steer one of the biggest stories in World Cup history. The English FA, by contrast, had five press officers, including one on 24-hour duty. Despite his official title, this was virgin territory for the association's press officer. 'Nobody could remember,' says the *Irish Times*, 'McKenna conducting a major press conference before.' Injury news, who trained, who sat and watched, a visit to a hospital by the players that afternoon. Oh and by the way . . . The text on the envelope had been tapped into a computer, and laser copies on FAI headed paper were handed around the media centre. Niall called Kennedy immediately, asking him to get to Roy before the players' statement did. It was too late. Unable to sleep, Roy had switched on Sky News in the wee hours to find footage of McKenna. He also saw highlights of Niall's press conference:

> I turn on the telly and Quinny is on giving his press conference.
> He's telling everyone what a week he has had. I'm at home and
> I'm saying to the telly, 'What a week you've had, Quinny?'

At the last and most farcical press conference of the day, Mick took issue with Niall's earlier remark that suggestions that the team had been given a him-or-me choice 'wouldn't be too far away'.

'Is that right? Well, I didn't give them an ultimatum. If the players wanted the situation reversed I would go with them.'

Convened at 8pm Izumo time, the press conference was abruptly truncated eleven minutes later by an obviously cagey General Secretary, Brendan Menton. Their intervening exchanges had been of Abbott-and-Costello proportions. Mick felt there were certain 'issues to be answered' and Menton, the perennial straight man, said that then was 'not the time'. Mick recalled how Roy 'lost his temper from the first second' and Menton interrupted nervously to the effect that 'the association doesn't want to revisit this, the timing of it, resurrecting itself'. The subtext being that Menton believed the deal to be still on and didn't want anything said that would scupper it.

Back in Cheshire, Kennedy was getting anyone he thought Roy would heed to call him. At 5pm Greenwich Mean Time, after a day of a thousand sways, Roy took his poor dog for yet another trot. The issue no longer seemed to be whether or not he would apologise and McCarthy would accept, but rather the unequivocal words of his former team-mates. Though Kennedy assured him that they hadn't been intended for release, he couldn't get them out of his head. When he got back, he called his solicitor and together they dressed the bitterness of his decision in regret and good wishes. 'The damage has been done,' he said.

I check the emails again first thing after breakfast. There is another from Paul in the Big Apple, and the last on this subject:

What a sad, sad end to it all. Will he ever be forgiven? Amazing that this is the week the FAI are getting their Euro 2008 bid together – shows where their heads have been the last few days. We'll all be watching it on Mexican telly. Here we (sort of) go. I hope Tommy still enjoys it.

25

Tommy thinks Roy is going to prison. He asks me on the evening of Wednesday the 29th. We are stalled at the lights on the square. I did wonder how a seven-year-old would come to grips with all this mayhem. After a week of seeing his hero being hounded through airports by reporters and cameramen, hearing the news on all channels referring to 'the disgraced Irish captain', it seems my son has concluded that Roy has done something else. He knows the bones of the official story, the one we tell him: Roy and Mick had a big row, after which Mick told Roy he didn't want him in his team any more. He just thinks that his parents are withholding the full truth. Roy did something we won't tell him about, like some crisis in the extended family we discuss over his head and describe as nothing when he asks. Now, after a week of bombardment, Tommy has concluded that there wasn't just a row. Roy did something really bad and is bound to pay the ultimate penalty.

'Dad?'

'Is Roy going to prison?'

'Prison!'

'Is he?'

I am laughing. Tommy isn't. He is embarrassed. I try to give it as much serious consideration as I can muster.

'Where did you hear that?'

'One of the bigger boys said it at school. He said Roy is in big trouble and is probably going to be put in prison.'

This is one twist even I didn't anticipate, but perhaps should have. Tommy has gone into the schoolyard, parroting his dad's summation for the defence. Most of the other lads have been handed at home the official match ball on which it is written 'Keane is a disgrace' and run so far with it as to reach the point where they are describing him as jailbait. There is a glimpse of our son in the bike shelter, getting shouted down. I try to assure Tommy that Roy didn't kill anybody. There was just a big row in which, it seems, Roy said some stuff he knows he shouldn't have said.

'Bad language?'

'I think so.'

'Really bad language?'

'I think so.'

'Like what?'

The lights go green.

'Arse?'

'Tommy.'

'Diddies?'

'*Thomas.*'

That night I overhear my wife on the phone to my mother. After we got back, Tommy grilled her about the nature of prison. Were you allowed up the town in the day, to go home at weekends? Was it true that you got locked into your room at night? In the end, he came to grips with the concept on his own terms.

'Are you allowed to take your teddies to bed?'

'Not sure about that one,' my wife said.

'Probably not,' Tommy decided. 'You're probably not allowed any teddies in prison.'

26

A midlands filling station in the heart of nowhere, the morning of Thursday the 30th. I have pulled over for a Diet Coke and prawn cocktail crisps. I'm standing at the counter when another customer breezes in and announces that he has just seen Roy Keane on the outskirts of Mullingar. The customer in question is male, in his late sixties. He looks like someone who took early retirement a few years ago and now considers it the decision of his life. He is quite well heeled. In short, he is not a hobo, nor does he strike me as someone given to sniffing solvents. The shop attendant asks, 'Where did you see him?'

'At the entrance to Atlantic Homecare,' the man says. 'He was driving in just as I was driving out.'

'How did you know it was him?'

'I was as close to him as I am to you. I pulled up alongside him and rolled down the window.'

'You pulled up alongside Roy Keane at the entrance to Atlantic Homecare?'

'Yes.'

'And what did he say?'

'Nothing.'

'*Nothing.* And what did you say?'

'I said, "You should have been man enough to apologise and I hope you're ashamed of yourself." '

'And what did Keane say to that?'

'Nothing.'

The country has been sprouting Roys all week. There haven't been so many unconfirmed sightings of one person since Elvis allegedly died. One contributor to the BBC Sport website even claims to have spotted Roy flogging the *Big Issue* on Royal Avenue in Belfast. Most have occurred understandably in Roy's native city, despite a vigil of hundreds at Cork Airport who believe that he isn't due to arrive until tomorrow. The newspapers have also featured several photos taken in Cork pubs of punters wearing Keano masks as a form of ongoing protest.

Even the Irish squad has its Roy impostors. According to Niall

Quinn, the official liaison officer between Umbro and the FAI John Fallon is renowned for his forgery of Roy's signature. First-choice keeper, Shay Given, does a great impersonation of his Mayfield squeal. Given and Damien Duff managed to make their captain laugh in Narita Airport by playing a comedy CD that included Keano impressions.

Arranmore Island off the coast of Donegal received a Charolais bull as a gift of the Irish Farmers' Association. The Bull Roy, expected to replenish a dwindling cattle herd, arrived yesterday on the daily ferry to a huge welcoming party. There was even a lone piper playing 'Let Erin Remember' on the pier. The island's IFA branch chairman expressed the wish that Arranmore was one island from which Roy would not be sent home. Elsewhere, sports columnist P.J. Cunningham says his second eldest recently came home despondent from school, having been told that he wouldn't be permitted to take 'Roy' as his Confirmation name. His choice was vetoed on the grounds that there is no 'St Roy'.

The most poignant phantom Roy appeared in a special World Cup supplement included free with the *Irish Independent* last Monday. Among those profiled was Brendan McKenna, the FAI press secretary. Read the day it came out and four days after Roy was sent home, it bristled with an optimism that seemed hopelessly redundant. McKenna said this World Cup was to have a special, 'additional' significance for his family. With the benefit of foresight, he surely would never have confided what he did:

My son Kevin and his wife Sinead are expecting their first child, and my first grandchild, on the eve of our opening game against Cameroon. The word is that if he's a boy he may be called 'Roy'.

27

The World Cup buster. We establish fifteen interested parties in the extended family and the sixteenth is made up of a syndicate of the four small grandchildren. We seed the thirty-two participating nations into two groups, and each party gets to draw one from each group. We put a fiver a man into a beautiful earthenware casserole dish our mother never uses and the one with the nation that lifts the trophy lifts €80.

We have given the seedings considerable time and thought. Are Sweden and Turkey, for example, really top-sixteen teams? Our collective pooled knowledge of African sides could fit inside a thimble. So Nigeria makes it into the upper echelon ahead of African champions, Cameroon. What's the word on Mexico? We rub our chins. Traditionally, we perpetuate history's grudge and demote England to the lower level. This year, however, their place is taken by Ireland. We simulate the dispassion of objectivity – dodgy centre-halfs, zilch in the middle of the park, no striker of proven international pedigree, shit manager – and lump Ireland in with Ecuador, Slovenia and other comical also-rans. It hurts.

Teatime on May the 30th, a Thursday and the day before the tournament's opening game. We have gathered in the kitchen at home to co-ordinate the draw. There is lots of slagging, but it's serious all the same. I have written in magic marker, in a childish simplistic hand, the names of sixteen countries on one A4 sheet and those of sixteen others on a second. Under the gaze of everyone else, I scissor the sheets into sixteenths of equal size and scrunch them into separate soup bowls. The kids are flapping and bouncing with excitement.

'Happy?'

In theory, everyone can expect to get one good team and one offering some entertainment value. For France 1998, for example, my younger brother drew Brazil to add to the flutter I placed on his behalf on France, so when it came to the final he was laughing. Yours truly, however, drew Bulgaria from the soup bowl marked 'Top Seeds'. The room cracked up. I tried to smile along, but my facial muscles were not playing ball. I tried to initiate a stewards' inquiry as to the competency of the seeding team. Considering that I was one third of the same seeding team, it didn't wash. Also, the seeding was influenced by performances at USA 1994, where Bulgaria had reached the semis and become folk heroes to the rest of Europe by eliminating Germany en route.

'Ummm, *Bulgaria*? Dark horses . . .'

'Piss off.'

We draw lots, 1–16, to establish the order. We go through the motions of the lower seeds. None of us wants Ireland. The previous two World Cups Ireland graced, we were tripping over each other to have the honour of wasting a fiver on Jack's warriors. Now it has emerged, in nods and grunts and stifled asides, that none of us could stomach having a vested interest as well as everything else. The only members of the buster to express a preference are the kids. So we have put a tiny green spot on one of the scraps in the 'Bottom Seed' and avoided it like the plague. They go 15, last but one. Their four faces peer into the bowl. I nod them towards the green spot. When the smallest hand makes a lunge towards the other piece of paper I give the bowl a sudden whirr.

'Take your time, take your time.'

Someone else at once asks and half answers a loud theatrical question.

'What two teams are left? Senegal and . . .'

They stand a second, staring quizzically at one another, before Tommy says, 'Ireland! Pick the one with the green spot. It's Ireland.'

As MC I insist on having the scrunched piece of paper handed to me. I unscrunch it, hold it face out and say in my best Sepp Blatter voice, 'Republic of Ireland!'

Their ecstasy is worth it. They go rushing to the end of the hall and back, cheering. They think they have pulled the stroke of the century on the rest of us. In the top seed draw they are under the misapprehension that Germany is a great coup. Nobody has the heart to tell them that this is regarded as the worst German side in decades. The rest are satisfied with their choices. I know what the last piece of paper in the bowl says when my turn comes. I wanted Italy but our mother got that. Brazil, France, Argentina, Spain, Portugal are all claimed. My bottom seeds are playing France in the opening game tomorrow lunchtime. We all laugh. I unscrunch my top seed and hold it up.

'Angleterre.'

28

'You'll never beat the Irish' may have become one of football's eternal truths, but there's a very good chance that you're not going to lose to them either.

Paul Howard, *The Gaffers*

The World Cup, as it turns out, is fairly successful, in a predictable sort of way. We play four matches, and three of those produce the same result, our favourite result: 1–1. We are the one-all specialists, the Brazilians of the moral victory. I can think of no other instance in which a footballing nation has patented and fetishised a particular scoreline. It has become the bequest of the Charlton/McCarthy years to Irish football. It has become Irish football's contribution to world football.

The pattern is almost always the same. They take an early lead. We show great character. We refuse to lie down. We eke out an equaliser, and leave it at that, point proven. There are no more chances between our goal and the final whistle. We raise our arms aloft, embrace. We go down to the end at which a sea of green is singing 'You'll never beat the Irish' and kiss our crests. The opposition have long since disappeared into the tunnel. Next day, they are pilloried in their tabloids, and we are lauded by the editorials of our broadsheets.

If I count correctly, Ireland has played twenty-three 1–1 draws since Jack Charlton took over as manager in March 1986. That pattern has its origins in the triptych of competitive matches against England played within a nine-month period in the early years of the Charlton reign. Remember those? The World Cup group match in Cagliari, June 1990. The home and away Euro 1992 qualifiers in November 1990, and March 1991. Each time they took the lead and each time John Motson sobbed, 'They've equalised.' We found in those stale dramas a renewable heroism, a parody of our troubled history with the old enemy.

I wonder if the average Irish fan actually prefers the 1–1 win to a consummate hammering of the opposition. Before leaving Manchester, Roy told Sir Alex that he felt we had a good chance of winning. Before flying home Mick, by contrast, will make much of the fact that we return from the World Cup 'undefeated', as if the word is the only equivalent of 'victorious' available to us. I even wonder if, in some unspoken way, we see the noble score draw as a workable metaphor for what being Irish means. It has everything we need. There is nothing of the stalemate of 0–0. Blood is drawn on both sides, and we get in the final blow. We also usually get the pleasure of anticipation, the satisfaction of knowing we fought back. Our point is a point saved, and we have none of the implicit guilt that all actual victories entail.

Our game against Holland in Italia 1990 was 1–1. Gullit scored a cracker in the first half. In the second, Packie Bonner hoofed it long, there was a clash of heads on the edge of the area, their keeper spilled it into Niall Quinn's path. Ron Atkinson called it 'an Irish one-two'. Word got through of England's winner against Egypt, and McCarthy and Gullit spent the last twenty minutes winking at each other. The game that got us to USA 1994, played against Northern Ireland amid palpable sectarian tension, was 1–1. It ruined the first dinner party my wife threw.

Sometimes, we get it wrong and make the mistake of scoring before them. 1–1 defeats don't feel quite so sweet. They recall Danny Blanchflower, Northern Ireland's skipper in Sweden 1958, who, juggling Protestant resolve and stage Irishry, said his side's only tactic was to equalise before the other side scored. Like Belgium at home in the play-off for France 1998, watched in a packed pub in central Dublin. By the end of the game I had not only a seat but a whole table to myself. Like Turkey at home in the play-off for Euro 2000. Like the home tie against Portugal in June of last year, when Roy forgot the script and for the rest of the second half his colleagues flustered around like chickens in green jerseys waiting for the axe to fall.

In Korea/Japan 2002, however, we lift the 1–1 win to an art form. Those games are like pre-ordained displays of brinkmanship. They feel like what it must have felt like watching Houdini live. Of the fightback against Cameroon, Niall Quinn will write: 'We take one all; we settle for that, happily, greeting the final whistle with joy.' That second penalty against Spain? It was as if the referee had allowed himself to become locked into the pattern of expectation. None of the Spanish players looked remotely surprised. Even I jump around for a few minutes. Niall again:

Ask me and I'd say it's the best Irish World Cup moment ever . . . For almost ten minutes, we carry on as if we've just won the World Cup.

29

Tommy and Eve are at that time of life when they could draw for Ireland. They have a vast collection of gel pens, in varying degrees of wastage, secreted in snap-lock sandwich bags and furry animal pencil cases in most rooms in the house. Every unplanned moment that in adolescence will be offered up to the all-consuming god of boredom gets filled with drawing. They draw in the car on journeys that take longer than twenty minutes, in the fitting rooms of Monsoon branches, on bookstalls during poetry readings. We have brokered a deal with them whereby they get tea in the Roma on Fridays and we sleep in undisturbed (blood injuries excepted) on Sundays. When one or both of us steps into the kitchen just in time to render 'Good morning' still admissible, they are silent on high stools at the island unit in their pyjamas. Their bowls half-full with soggy Coco Pops have been pushed into the centre and they are drawing.

Eve draws patterns mostly, no figurative representation discernable and no colour in her palette spared. I ask her, stupidly, what it's *of* and she answers, 'It's of colours.' When she does choose to draw someone and/or something, even money says it will be herself, the sun will be shining and the clouds in the dark-blue sky will look suspiciously like the sheep in the lime-green fields. Tommy confines himself to football. All winter the house has been littered with unfinished Liverpool crests and pictures of Michael Owen's back. He interrupts the creative impulse to ask his old man what the score was between us and United in Old Trafford the year before last.

'Can we go on the computer later to find out?'

'Sure.'

Then he's back at the coffee table in the sitting room, tongue hugging his top lip, leaning into a blank page pinched from the printer in the guest room and a sticker book lying spreadeagled for reference. Predictably, in the past few weeks, mere club colours have taken a back seat. The pages have been decorated with tricolours and Roy has scored goal after good-humoured goal in every corner in the house. An old decommissioned phone book is kept in the desk in their bedroom. Its international dialling code pages prove useful for the book of flags of all the participating nations in the World Cup they are making. Just out of the bath, I pause on the landing on the way to our room and eavesdrop on the production process. Eve, disenchanted, is asking, 'Why do I get all the crap countries?'

'Ecuador aren't crap,' her brother is telling her. 'Ecuador are brilliant.'

'I want to do Brazil.'

'Evie, I've done Brazil.'

'Then I want to do France.'

'I've done France as well. Look. You can do Costa Rica.'

'I'm telling. You get all the good countries and I get all the crap ones.'

Her stockinged footsteps approach the other side of the door and stop.

'*Evie*! You can do . . . England.'

'Can I?'

'Yeah. You can.'

'Are they good?'

'They're brilliant. They're probably going to win.'

After school on Friday the 31st. Tommy presents me with a black-and-white line drawing of Roy on the plane from Saipan to Manchester. He is in the cabin on his own, lounging on a very large seat. He has his feet up on a stool. The mug of hot tea in his hand has three concentric cows' licks of steam billowing from it. He is watching a match on the telly that's perched on a second stool. You can tell from the grin on his freckled face how glad he is to be heading home and how clear his conscience is. The handful of hairs on his head are standing to attention. The football boots on his feet look suspiciously like mice and he still hasn't seen fit to change out of his Ireland strip. Through each of the six portholes you can glimpse what looks like the same single snow-capped peak in the distance. A big Bakelite rotary dial phone, complete with pig's tail, is ringing silently on the dumbwaiter beside him.

'Thank you.'

'Will you frame it?'

'Uh huh.'

'Is that a yes?'

'Yes.'

'I thought so.'

This, for the rest of the World Cup, is the last drawing by Tommy in which Roy will feature. It is, I will come to realise, a kind of parting gift. The parting, of course, is not actual. We will breakfast at the same table for the rest of the summer and, I hope, the rest of the decade at least. But from this moment, when he sits alone in a Lear jet with a mug of tea and a phone rattling, Roy is mine and my generation's to sentimentalise. The next time I peer over Tommy's shoulder at the island unit he will become embarrassed and ratty, as if I somehow disapprove of his new heroes.

30

Of all ex-players, Paul McGrath has been the least equivocal in his support of Roy. On national radio last Friday morning, the show that was twittering in the postman's van, Paul wasn't pulling his punches. 'I'm on Roy's side in all this,' he said. 'He's pulled us through this competition and he's got us to the finals.' He was 'shattered', 'devastated' and the whole affair was 'wrecking [his] head'. He also smelt conspiracy in the haste of Colin Healy's call-up. Other than that, however, Paul's interpretation of the squad meeting is brilliantly simple. Mick, having asked Roy what he thought, sent Roy home because Roy told him what he thought:

> The manager has asked him questions he obviously wanted answered straight, and he got the answers straight. Why should Mick conduct all his dealings with Roy in front of every other player and then ask questions he knows Roy is going to answer straight? . . . [Roy's] voiced his opinion and he's been vilified for it.

The bond between Paul and Roy has always fascinated me. They are friends, or seem to be. When *The Late Late Show* had a tribute to Paul, Roy was in the audience and Paul singled him out. There have been sightings of the pair of them in the stands at Anfield, watching Paul's son play for Liverpool Youths. According to Paul, he and Mick 'didn't have a great relationship'. By contrast, he spoke with Roy on the phone two days before the squad flew out to Saipan. Roy, he said, was upbeat and couldn't wait for it to start.

More than just a bond, Paul and Roy are like flip sides of a single coin. It is as if each is the person and player the other could have become. Both played League of Ireland and were unusually old when they crossed the Irish Sea. They have similar introverted temperaments, dodgy career-threatening knees and alleged histories of 'depression'. I insert inverted commas because that's how it gets pronounced, as if meant as a euphemism for an altogether darker condition. What Paul, on the radio last week, termed his 'situation'.

It may be broad to assume that Paul's 'situation' is the same as Roy's, but from the outside looking in they look remarkably similar. Both have admitted needing a jar to overcome certain social obstacles. Ferguson has always claimed that booze, and the player's inability to kick it, was central to the decision to sell Paul. At one point during the 1997/8 season, the other United players were forbidden from drinking with Roy who was recovering from his cruciate ligament operation. Starting at the same point, back to back, they have walked in opposite directions. Paul is spotted occasionally on benders in Dublin. Roy has all the club medals you can win in a bank vault and his abstinence, in Paul Hayward's memorable phrase, has rendered him 'a remote and gloomy figure, pounding country lanes'.

For all his failings, perhaps *because* of his failings, Paul remains the most loved of all Irish footballers. Attitudes to Paul and Roy in Ireland are similar to those to Garrincha and Pele in Brazil. Garrincha and Pele played in two World Cups together. When the former died of alcohol abuse, leaving three wives and thirteen children destitute, the latter's name was a registered trademark. 'But while Brazilians put Pele on a pedestal,' Alex Bellos writes in *Futebol: The Brazilian Way of Life*, 'they do not *love* him the way they love Garrincha.' Everyone in Ireland has an affectionate first-name relationship with Paul. He is 'Paul', or 'Big Paul', but never 'McGrath'. Half of the football-loving nation have only recently learned to tolerate, but never warmed to, 'Keane'.

Now Paul is Ireland's latest World Cup casualty. He has been sent home from Japan as well, for his own tirade. He was to be part of the BBC commentary team. He flew over yesterday on a flight that was also carrying the wives and families of the Irish squad. It had already been a turbulent trip. The plane got stuck in Stockholm for two hours, having collided with the cargo truck that was to load its in-flight meals. Also, Irish players were getting furious calls from their spouses, complaining that only one of the toilets was working and that there were no movies. Then, according to reports, Paul put icing on the cake in the form of abuse hurled at the wife of a 'prominent player'. Several reports suggest that he had been drinking and that the subjects under discussion were Roy and Saipan. 'In the light of his recent behaviour,' a spokeswoman said, 'the BBC and Paul agreed that he should return to the UK.' Now the most loved of all Irish footballers is in the air again, and I await Tommy's drawing.

31

Argentina 1978. The first summer that international football crossed my horizon. We didn't qualify. We didn't come close. Instead, we all supported Scotland and left the front lawn threadbare with kickabouts between matches. My eldest brother thumped the third in line for letting a soft goal in. His knuckles cut on my other brother's lower teeth and turned septic. He spent a week in hospital. Our mother got her hair permed like Mario Kempes.

Just as the opening game was kicking off, a posse of strangers from Chicago, claiming to be our cousins, landed on my grandparents' step next door. There is a photograph the Yanks took of all of us lined in our grandparents' living room, with freckles the size of halfpennies. In the background you can just about make out live coverage of holders West Germany and Poland in the opening game. The eldest of the visitors said to my grandfather, 'These guys sure love their soccer, huh?'

Like everybody else, the game I remember most is Scotland's with Holland, in which they had to win by three clear goals: Archie Gemmill – 'a hard little professional' – momentarily becoming George Best; the impossible looking probable until Johnny Repp popped one from what looked like 80 yards. I didn't see any of it, at least not live. Just as the ref was putting the whistle to his lips, me and a kid from four doors up (who is now a gynaecologist) got into a scrap in our front room. For the record, I gave him a shiner. We all got sent to bed. My brothers blamed me for the rest of the tournament, and have never let me forget it.

I could understand why I got the red card, but why my brothers did as well was for years beyond me. In fact, it occurs to me that we got sent to bed very easily, and with great frequency. So I asked our mother the other day and she started laughing. Our father invariably came home mid-evening, three sheets to the wind and fell asleep on the bed. She would use any excuse to send us to bed and get all the curtains of the house closed. When he woke around ten, intent on more, to a house silent and in darkness, he thought it was the wee hours and rolled over. We were wide awake in our rooms, standing at the ends of our beds in pyjamas, peering out into daylight and wondering what it was we had done that was so terrible.

32

He was for Ireland and Parnell and so was his father.
James Joyce, *A Portrait of the Artist as a Young Man*

It is the first World Cup Tommy will remember. In time to come, this will hold the same place in his memory that Argentina 1978 holds in mine. He has learned his history, the dates and host nations. He asks if Ireland played well in Argentina, and can't really get his little head around the concept of Italia 1990 as our Book of Genesis. I explain it again, slowly, and he squints at that thought as if at the glare of blank Antarctic space. The evening before the opening match against Cameroon, he cashes €5 of his savings stamps in the post office and buys a huge Tesco tricolour.

So I fake it for his sake. There is a passage in Ian Hamilton's wonderful *Gazza Agonistes* where he talks about the misgivings you experience watching your national side get along without your player, the one you daydreamed would score a late winner to eliminate the defending champions:

When England played well without Hoddle, I took a diminished pleasure in their triumph. What it chiefly signified to me, and my co-worshippers, was that Glenn would not be in the team next week. On the other hand, if Glenn had played, had made the winning goal, our patriotic joy would have been boundless . . . And it was much the same with Jimmy Greaves. How many Greaves fans, I wonder, wholeheartedly savoured that 1966 World Cup win? Greaves didn't. He left the stadium immediately after the presentations and skipped the banquet afterwards. How could we not skip it too?

But I go through the motions all the same, because I don't think it would be fair to Tommy not to. I set the alarm for the early kick-off, give his nibs a stir and sit beside him on the edge of the coffee table. We're both shivering; nerves and first-light chill in equal parts. He is living every minute of it, kick by kick, and I am approximating the right noises from memory.

When Cameroon are running rings around us for the first half, I do a lot of head-shaking. I manage not to cheer when they hit the front not long before the whistle, or to appear too buoyant during the break. Then I suffer as 'our lads' battle back. When Matt Holland equalises and Barry Davies gloats 'it couldn't come from a nicer fella' I muster a loud handclap and a half-hearted *Yes*. The rest is a blur, spent on my feet between the kitchen and the telly. By the time the ref blows it up, I know there will be too much crowing. So I hit the standby button and resume the Saturday morning lie-in.

That night, or maybe the night after, Tommy asks about Mr Roy Keane. He means the rag doll my mother gave him for his birthday last month. Truth to tell, Mr Roy Keane was originally a Ms. My mother took the scissors to its mane of golden hair and Tommy didn't ask awkward questions. Now, but for its ear-to-ear smile, it could pass for Johnny Rotten in an Ireland strip of a dodgy shade of green. For some reason it has had the full formal handle from day one.

He wants to know what he should call Mr Roy Keane now that the real Roy has gone home. I say, 'Promise me you'll always call him Mr Roy Keane.'

'Why?'

'Because Roy's the greatest player ever to play for Ireland, and they wouldn't be in the World Cup but for him.'

'Promise.'

'Promise.'

'Promise.'

33

Great 1–1 Wins in Irish History:
The English Triptych, Part I

In June 1990 myself and my new girlfriend were renting a farmer's cottage in rural Co. Meath. She was working as a pre-season tour guide on a megalithic tomb and I was along for the ride. By the morning of Saturday, 11 June, I was already feeling the heat. That was the day of our first ever World Cup finals game. We had prayed for this, collectively, for decades and now it had arrived.

Whatever nerves we had were multiplied by the fact that it was England. History and football do not mix. There had been the glory of our 1–0 win against them in Stuttgart 1988, but even those ninety-odd minutes had taken too great a toll to want to relive them in the same lifetime. The draw had been as much a horror for England. You could see it on Bobby Robson's face in Rome in December of the previous year. We had watched the ceremony in darkest Donegal, in the most northerly pub in Ireland. There was no telly in the front bar and I was the only one on the premises who was aware or cared that the draw was happening. So they opened the disco especially and plugged in the big screen. We sat on stools in the middle of the dance floor, nursing hot whiskeys. When our name was drawn third for Group D, behind Holland and England, my groans were so loud that a row of suspicious faces peered around the partition and I felt obliged to apologise.

We hitched to my family home to see the match. We got a lift to the main road from members of the Orange Order on a reconnaissance mission to suss out the site of the Battle of the Boyne for their tricentenary celebrations. As we were getting out, they asked me to point them towards the north-west. I, out of routine sectarian mischief, pointed them towards the south-east and said to drive a good two hours in that direction. A private bus from town pulled up and the driver wouldn't take any money. All that half-hour, standing in the aisle, I had this guilty image flitting through my head of two starched Church of Ireland gentlemen, hitting yet another unmarked crossroads in the wilds of Co. Wexford.

And the game? A sorry affair. We have forgotten, by sheer force of nostalgia, just how awful Italia 1990 really was. We didn't win a single game in normal time, scored two goals from open play and somehow found ourselves vying with the host nation for a place in the semi-final against Maradona and Argentina. England took the lead, true to the script. Gary Lineker got the credit. Gazza and Waddle did an Irish jig in front of the benches. At half-time my mother served what she usually served on St Patrick's Day: spuds, peas, turnip, chop (all the colours of the tricolour, plus brown). Then Steve McMahon came on and we were all square. I still feel sorry for Steve and his fame by default in Irish football history. He got the nod with twenty left on the clock and a lead still to protect. He got booked. He lost the ball twice in quick succession in his own half, the second time to Kevin Sheedy and we have loved Kevin ever since.

The last ten minutes was one long knowing smile on the lips of Bobby Robson. What did Bobby *know*, exactly, that he smiled so much against us? Sometimes Bobby looked as if he was smiling because this had all been part of his master plan, a trap into which we had blundered, by scoring. More often, however, his smile looked like the sanguine smirk of one who felt turned over by Lady Luck once again, in circumstances so perverse as to become a running joke. A further irony was added by the fact that his new nemesis was also his fellow Geordie, Jackie Charlton. Calling Big Jack 'Jackie' was Bobby's way of reminding us that he was England's long before he was ours, and you couldn't blame him for that. After the game in Cagliari the two embraced on the pitch with all the relief of friends who had not ruined each other's chances.

After the game, we piled into the car and drove downtown to be among the action. The square was black. They were blaring car horns and waving flags. We did the loop of three streets at least a dozen times, just so we could cruise at 5mph through the square once more, holding raised palms out the window to be shook and slapped by all the people lined along the traffic islands. There was even a group of teenage lads splashing in the fountain. Colchester and Barnsley were probably deserted, the pubs humming with recriminations. Where both countries had emerged with one goal and one point, we became one big remake of La Dolce Vita and all England was calling it a night earlier than usual.

34

Tommy has been on the telly, we think. For a couple of years he's been sending drawings into RTÉ's afternoon slot for kids, The Den, with no success. Then, on the morning of 4 June 2002, the Tuesday after our first game, he gets a jiffy bag in the post. He gets post so rarely that he's stunned to see it on the table, unopened, when he comes down for breakfast. He gets post only on his birthday, and initially seems a bit confused. Inside there is a baseball cap, a notebook, a few stickers and a T-shirt that won't fit him until around the age he starts shaving – all black and all with the programme logo on it. They must have used his most recent masterpiece, since anyone who gets their picture shown wins a goody bag. He takes it into school for news. When we're walking home, I ask him to describe the picture. He says it was of Roy's Ireland jersey, with the number and the Cameroon match details on the breast and the captain's armband on one sleeve. I remember it. It was slightly flared, the short sleeves were very short indeed and the Umbro logo was oversized to the point where it bled into the '6'. The backdrop was blank, as if the jersey Roy would have worn last Saturday had been laid out onto new-fallen snow. His mother posted it.

Dustin the Turkey, the puppet sidekick to *The Den*'s perennially youthful continuity announcer, is getting a roasting. Dustin is the turkey/builder with the abrasive Dublin accent who has topped the Irish music charts with pop songs rehashed to 'funny' lyrics. More often than not Dustin sports a United jersey, so it should come as no great shock that he voiced his support for Roy. The show's website has been inundated with ripostes from angry seven-year-olds. A selection occasionally gets read on air. They reek of parental supervision. It sounds as if the question 'Mam, how do you spell *treason*?' has been heard in a thousand Irish houses in the past few days.

The director of the ISPCC says that a huge number of kids are understandably traumatised, and advises parents to use what newspapers are calling 'The Keane Crisis' as an 'opportunity to talk to kids about the nature of conflict, about disappointment'. They are saying exam results will drop this year. The founder of the Personal Counselling Institute has warned that 'the precious time for study and revision is being impinged upon by the unfolding drama in the Far East.' The Samaritans have been flooded with calls over the weekend, most from teenagers linking their respective shades of blue to Roy Keane. One father, bearing in mind the time difference, even called the *Irish Times* office at 2am on Tuesday the 28th. He seriously asked if there had been any happy developments in Japan he could tell his nine-year-old who wasn't sleeping.

I read that and wonder about my own son. He seems grand. But you never know. The biggest danger, as the Samaritans' spokesman said, is bottling it up. So I ask him over breakfast later that week if he's okay. True to form, it ends up arseways.

'I'm grand,' he says.

'You're not still bothered about Roy?'

'Roy Keane?'

'Yes, *Roy Keane*.'

'Nah.'

'Good man. Because you know if ever you want to talk . . .'

'I'm grand. What about you, Dad?'

'Grand.'

'Sure?'

'Still a bit depressed about the whole thing.'

'*Depressed?*'

'Sad.'

'Right.'

'I mean, if McCarthy had handled it better, if he hadn't called a team meeting at all, if he just sorted it between the two of them, and if Roy could've just put his head down and soldiered on . . .'

He puts his small arm around my shoulder.

'It'll be grand,' he says.

'Thanks.'

'And if ever you fancy a chat you know where I am.'

'Thanks.'

35

Great 1–1 Wins in Irish History:
The English Triptych, Part II

In November 1990 I had a brain tumour. Mine wasn't the kind of brain tumour that got merely *diagnosed*. My brain tumour was the result of intuition: I just knew. I had, it's true, gone to some quack and it was all he could do to stifle the initial tremors of a giggle. He shone a pinhead light into my pupils, wrote 'hypochondria' into medical records the width of a telephone directory and prescribed sinus decongestants.

In those days I treated my doctors the way most young writers treat their women. I appeared out of nowhere, wooed them with the quality of my indifference, spoiled them with a flurry of unscheduled visits and then, when it had started feeling predictable or they had just stopped listening, I dropped them. At that point the analogy begins to wear thin. Each new flame is not glancing back and forth between you and a dossier of previous complaints. I swapped doctors frequently, hoping I would at last get taken seriously. Then, on the desk of each fresh surgery I stepped into, shaking hands and declaring my 'profession', my past had arrived before me and had already snitched.

Dr Savage was different. He was an enormous GP from the midlands whose pad was at the end of the road on which myself and my latest flame had just taken a basement flat. He had the look of a country vet who had been awarded the wrong qualifications and could never stir himself enough to point out the mistake. When he should have been on the Longford–Roscommon border, with his good arm up the rear end of a mare, he found himself in a dilapidated Victorian house on the north side of Dublin city centre, looking at an unemployed writer who had diagnosed his own imminent death.

Dr Savage's demeanour was the most doleful I have ever come across. I realise now that you could have gone to him with ingrowing toenails and stepped out believing your end was nigh, as I did after my appointment on the afternoon of 14 November. I had found the symptoms hard to put into actual words: not dull 'headaches' as such, more sudden stabs of pain; a general 'fuzziness' and lack of co-ordination, especially early in the morning.

'Hmmm,' he said eventually in his weight-of-the-world way. 'Yeah.'

He spread his hands across my skull, asked me to wiggle my fingers at eye level and pressed the nib of his ballpoint into one of my cheekbones.

'Is that sore?'

'Yes.'

He said it could be serious. Unable to meet my eye, he said we would have to get tests, soon. He might as well have covered his head with black sackcloth as he spoke. He told me to go home and expect a call in the next forty-eight hours about an appointment. There was nobody there. My girlfriend had done the unthinkable: she had got a job. And as if to compound my problems, the home game against England had kicked off and it wasn't even on the telly. There were still no floodlights in Landsdowne Road, so even Wednesday internationals were played in the middle of the afternoon. Wrangling over broadcast rights meant that I had to listen to it on my grandfather's eight-band Grundig wireless, the way he and his brothers had done for decades, picturing the action in my ailing head. Of the four competitive internationals against England in that general period, therefore, this made the least impression.

A textbook 1–1, insofar as any of us remember. Who took the

lead for England? Who equalised for us? Most punters in any football pub can recite scorers' names and goal times of Irish internationals, the way their ancestors could rattle off the rosary. But the home qualifier against England for Sweden 1992? Subsequent accounts say we should have won. We should have put away, in our own back yard, a team we had the wood over. But we couldn't, and we couldn't bring ourselves to say as much in the post-match quotes. So the game got filed under 'Glorious Comebacks' and promptly forgotten. David Platt and Tony Cascarino. I don't think I have ever witnessed either strike. The news didn't even have the rights to show clips, and yet sometimes I think I can visualise them.

I killed the applause and lay down on the couch. There were no car horns on the road, no fountains in danger. A degree of Ireland–England fatigue had set in. I lay for a few hours in sickening light, taking comfort from the main evening news reports of the Gardaí baton-charging English fans down Parnell Street. There was a power cut that evening. I bought chips and a can of Harp for tea, and ate them by candlelight. I wasted a couple of weeks expecting the axe to fall. I never got called by any hospital. I have since wondered if Dr Savage had been put up to it by some doctor's guild, under instructions to scare me off once and for all. It worked. I got a job of sorts shortly after and the country was never the same again.

36

Germany, 5 June 2002. Time was when the day of a big Ireland match got wasted pacing the back garden and gazing at empty space. For the first time since my early twenties, when I fell head over heels in love, football this weather has acquired a numb aura from which I feel oddly removed. It means little or nothing to me. I imagine that I have been having one of those out-of-body experiences described by people who have died and come back again, and are able to describe floating above themselves while the medics are attempting to jolt their hearts to life.

It is a school day. The match is due to kick off at noon, and the kids have been promised they can watch it in the gym hall. Last night, together, Tommy and me pinched a bamboo stake from one of his mother's rose bushes and attached it to his tricolour to bring into school. My wife knows the score. She thinks it's funny, but this morning pretends to be suspicious about the origins of his flagpole. She is acting a part for Tommy, allowing him to feel he has taken his place among the men. We wink and make faces behind her back, like two amigos off to shout for the auld sod. His tricolour is easily the biggest. His classmates stop in their tracks and gasp 'Cool, cool.'

My younger brother comes over. He works close by and grants himself an extended lunch. He buys two breakfast rolls on the way and I brew fresh coffee. It's been a fair while since we watched Ireland games in the same room. These days, we usually stick to separate bases and confer at half- and full-time. But his take on the whole Roy debacle has been much the same as mine, and his being here at all suggests that this means less.

They go in front, thanks to a Pole ghosting in between our two centre-halfs. The Germans are no great shakes. We reach the break one down. We always do. I collect Eve because her class gets out an hour before Tommy's and when we get back Bobby Robson in the ITV studio is referring to Ireland in the first person plural. Steven Staunton is replaced by Kenny Cunningham in the eighty-seventh minute. We have had our chances. Then, with ninety-two minutes up, Steve Finnan launches one last hurrah from halfway. You know the rest.

Our cheer is so abrupt and surprising, even to ourselves, that Eve bursts into tears. She sobs on my knee while John Motson shouts, 'You can't say they don't deserve it, you can't say they don't deserve it.'

Today is a special day for Dundalk. Staunton becomes the first Irish footballer to receive a hundred international caps. Half the town takes to the street this evening, just like old times. We can hear cheering and car horns beeping from our back door.

37

Great 1–1 Wins in Irish History:
The English Triptych, Part III

The game with England on 27 March 1991 is remembered as the apogee of the 1–1 win. It gets dusted down occasionally and repeated with the flimsiest excuse, in a manner that would be laughable at the BBC. Why this above all others? Perhaps because it remains our most recent competitive game with England, and has settled in our heads as the point at which the Stuttgart advantage was kept intact. Because it was Wembley, the lions' den. Because they took the lead through a Staunton o.g. and, although the spoils were technically shared, we have had the satisfaction of knowing that both goals came from an Irish boot. Because Kevin Moran had his head split open, fought on heroically in a turban and even hit the post. Because our favourite son, Paul McGrath, conducted the orchestra.

I watched it in the sitting room of the house at home. It was a Wednesday night and I had got the bus up to visit my mother. She had just had a hysterectomy and was camped in the spare bedroom at the end of the hall because she couldn't go upstairs. We sat in silence for the first twenty minutes. Niall Quinn equalised just when it looked as if they were going to hold out until half-time. Roddy Doyle called Niall's celebration, a nonchalant windmill of the right arm while running away to the corner flag, the most stylish in Irish football history. We made such a racket that a friend of my mother's who was on bedside duty came down the hall to tell us to have some consideration.

In the interval prattle Jimmy Hill asked Terry Venables, 'Would the Right Honourable Member for Tottenham kindly remind me which side is playing at home?' Lee Sharpe made his international debut. Ray Houghton was clean through with ten minutes to go. The country was on its knees, inches from our screens, when his shot hit the wrong side of the net and Jack pulled his cap down over his eyes. Ray has since said that he gets ribbed about that miss more often than he gets congratulated for the goals he didn't miss. I caught the early train next morning.

It occurs to me that that night would not have become so embedded in our memory if we had won. The win would always have been eclipsed by Stuttgart. The emphasis, then, was on protecting rather than stretching the advantage. The games in Cagliari and Dublin had been so poor. Finally we had a 1–1 win of which we could be truly proud. Although Jack's actual retirement was still four and a half years away, Wembley, March 1991 was its beginning. A late equaliser in Poland by Gary Lineker saw to it that Sweden 1992 was the first major tournament Jack's green army didn't grace. The team he had built was ageing and the country's expectations were changing. There was already talk of a young tearaway from Cork who had just been awarded the Barclay's Young Eagle of the Month for February and whose international debut was only two months around the corner.

38

In Cork, Roy is God. He is the uncrowned king.

Con O'Leary, Cork City Council

The capital of the Rebel County has remained faithful to its favourite son throughout all the fuss. All website postings and letters in newspapers with Cork addresses have taken his side. The City Council sent an official letter of solidarity to Cheshire. Street trade in Keano memorabilia has gone through the roof. A sports store in the city centre claimed that its sales of the Ireland No. 6 jersey increased by 400 per cent, although admittedly that could mean that they sold four this week as opposed to one last week. A pair of the great man's boots went for €3,000 in a charity auction held the night before Ireland's opening game.

In his interview for RTÉ with Tommy Gorman he had said, 'I want to be able to walk down Patrick Street in Cork with my head held high.' He finally caught up with Dr John Buckley after his decision not to fly back had been announced. 'He told me he was delighted with the support of the people of Cork,' the Bishop later remarked, 'and was looking forward to spending a few days at home.' But when? Fans kept vigil at Cork Airport for three days from Wednesday, 29 May. A group of Mayfield schoolgirls erected a giant banner that read 'We Love You Roy'. By lunchtime on Friday the 31st rumours of his imminent arrival, not via the VIP exit but through the usual arrivals gate like you or I, had swelled the vigil to several hundreds.

They were, of course, to be disappointed. He didn't arrive on the Friday lunchtime, and by tea word was that he had acceded to a request from his immediate family to leave it for a bit. His mother and father had spent the previous weekend locked into their holiday home in West Cork, besieged by reporters and photographers. They feared that having their son himself on the manor would prompt a second wave of media hysteria. Instead, he touched down on the late flight from Manchester on the night of Monday, 3 June. The vigil had dispersed, and his seat had been reserved so late that his name didn't appear on the passenger list. He slipped through Arrivals virtually unnoticed, was met by a friend of the family, driven to the Templeacre Tavern, sipped one rock shandy and signed autographs outside for ten minutes.

His family was right. For the four nights their son was home, their house was surrounded once again by local paparazzi. He signed so many posters and jerseys that there must have been moments when a whole new injury – writer's cramp – seemed likely to enter his already extensive medical scrapbook. It was reported that he intended to watch the Germany match with his family. On Wednesday the 5th, the evening after the match, he lost his rag with one photographer. Donna McBride, who last November became the first female press photographer to work in Iran when she travelled with the Irish squad, called to collect some shots she had taken at the award ceremony of his honorary degree and had left with his parents to get autographed. 'I couldn't believe the response I got,' Donna said. 'He was very rude and warned me that this was private property and I should get out. He got all the photos and shoved them at me.'

Whether his foul mood was a result of Ireland's result or press harassment is uncertain. What is certain is that he cuts short his trip home and flies back at 8.30am on Friday the 7th, as ever signing caps and boarding passes on the way. His humour has improved. 'I have to say I thought he was lovely,' one woman whose children had approached him tells the papers. He flits through the departure gate and completely vanishes off the radar for six weeks.

39

Our telly has gone on the blink. We got it as a wedding gift from one of my older brothers nine years ago. Up until then we hadn't had one for a couple of years, and considered this new addition a mixed blessing. We had stopped considering ourselves telly people. We liked what not having a telly said about us. We took perverse pleasure in the knowledge that any members of either side of the extended family who slept over would return to the hills with hair-raising tales of our tellyless flat.

I think nobody would have dared buy us one as a gift, but for the fact that we had finally tied the knot. It was as if the telly represented recognition within the family that my new wife and I were making sincere attempts to be *normal*. We deserved encouragement. Gradually, however, we managed to make it our telly. We invested in a set of rabbits' ears that picked up nothing more than Ireland's two terrestrial channels and, stuck to the top of the box with suction pads, looked a show. We propped it on a stool bought in a shop selling the produce of occupational therapy for recovering alcoholics, made much of the fact that it and we existed miraculously without a solitary zapper. Somewhere in the intervening decade the door that hid the tuning buttons dropped off. That tiny part of both of us that remains unreconstructed bohemian still gets a kick out of the horror on the faces of 24-inch flat wide-screen digital friends who drop by.

Tuesday, 11 June 2002. Today we take on the sheikhs of Saudi Arabia for a place in the last sixteen. All weekend the colour on our nine-year-old telly has been getting increasingly temperamental. On Saturday Tommy and me had made toast, sat on the couch in pyjamas at midday to watch Brazil's second Group C game against

China. China, their white strip rendered suddenly emerald, looked like extras from *Darby O'Gill and the Little People*. The classic canary yellow of Brazil became the luminous orange of council workers in their overalls. Initially, normal colour service could be resumed by giving the box the merest clip on the ear. Portugal against Poland yesterday: one's red tops and green shorts became black and darker green; the other's white tops and red shorts became green and black. It was impossible to tell the teams apart. At one point Jerzy Dudek seemed to roll the ball out to one of the opposition's centre forwards, and Figo was scythed down by his own team-mates. By then it was a joke no amount of clattering would undo.

Today, World Cup fever has hit the kids' school. They are let out early to watch the match. Tommy is disgusted with his old man, since his old man promised to get the telly either seen to or replaced by this lunchtime. Now he returns in uniform to find that Ireland are the All Blacks attempting to put away a team kitted out suspiciously like, well, Ireland.

'If Roy Keane was playing,' he complains, 'you'd get it fixed.'

This is the first intimation that my son is browned off with his father's pro-Roy bias. It is also, of course, not a million miles wide of the mark. The deterioration of our box is directly proportional to this co-owner's recent and increasing disinterest in international football. The prospect of a squabble is averted when Keane the younger, Robbie, puts us in front after only eight minutes. A long pass into the corner by local hero, a cross deflected high into the floodlit Yokohama evening and buried before it reaches the deck on its way back down.

'Is that us?'

There is one extraordinary moment immediately after. Robbie has found time to work on his goal celebrations. For today's showdown he has come up with a kind of Robin Hood imitation: the archer's stance, the left holding the bow out front and the right letting the wire go in a sudden four-fingered fan. Every time he gets himself in position to fire he is mobbed by another team-mate just arriving on the scene. They want to say 'Well done my son', and he is furiously wrestling them away so he can do his bow-and-arrow bit.

I start lunch, aware of the muted noises from the next room. I put my head through with twenty minutes on the clock. No change. The lull in which me and my wife eat at the kitchen table is punctuated by the sounds of Tommy groaning 'Get rid of it,' and Eve's little moth-voice saying 'Oh no, oh no . . .' My wife thinks my presence at the table is politeness.

'Go on in and eat it off your lap,' she keeps saying.

'I'm grand.'

Half-time.

'Who do you hope wins, Dad?'

'Us, of course.'

I have my fingers crossed. I manage to phrase it in such a way that I know will sound like what he wants to hear, and about which he will not go to the bother of thinking twice.

'Us. I hope we win.'

'Me too. C'mon Ireland.'

The second half picks up where the first left off. They are coming at the Irish defence thick and fast. An embarrassment seems well on the cards. Tommy's questions are coming like rapid fire as well.

'Are Saudi Arabia good?'

'Are Saudi Arabia better than us?'

'Do you think the ref is crap?'

'Has it ever happened that a goalie has gone to kick the ball out, missed it and knocked it into the goal with his foot coming back down?'

Then Gary Breen, the centre-half, scores. He looks like the Incredible Hulk.

'Who scored? Is that one-all?'

I have warmed to Gary. An Irish cockney who has recently seen

Coventry go down, he is one of those vulnerable, unreliable journeymen for whom it is hard not to harbour a soft spot. He and David Connolly went up to Roy's room to say they agreed with everything he said; to say they were sorry for not speaking out, but that they refused to join the round of applause in support of Mick. Damien Duff makes it three when their keeper, who has looked all night like an octopus in a tracksuit, flaps it into his own net.

David, my wife's sister's son, calls before full time. The rest of the family are in Egypt and he has the keys to the castle for two weeks. I think he is feeling the absence of anybody to discuss tactics with or share high fives. He calls and, his luck being what it is, gets me on the cordless in apron on the sofa.

'Yeah, they're great,' I say. '*Great.*'

I launch into Lee Carsley who has just come on. A sort of poor man's Roy, Carsley has been one of McCarthy's pets over the past few seasons and my favourite whipping boy. I managed to contain my contempt for him up until the first leg of the play-off with Turkey for Euro 2000, when we were looking down the barrel at a precious home win before Carsley nominated himself keeper and slapped the ball away from the feet of Hakan Sukur. 1–1. Today, in lieu of a gold watch, he gets a last-minute gallop and a slap on the back from Mick.

The end of the line is silent. Poor David. There he is on his own, calling in the hope of some breezy mutual congratulation, and getting an earful. He is right. Roy is no more as far as this World Cup, as far as the Irish team is concerned. There and then I resolve to smile and join the party, to be a killjoy no longer. They're saying it will be Spain and somehow it seems easier to be a well-wisher in the face of certain elimination. I spend the rest of the evening practising my golf swing out the back and going through Tommy's four nightly spelling words – *cramp, shamrock, many, anything.*

40

Sir,
Grumpy Dunphy sat on a wall
Grumpy Dunphy had a great fall
All Keane's horses and all Keane's men
Will never put Dunphy together again.
Yours etc,
Donal Walsh,
Blackrock.

Irish Times, 5 June 2002

The weeks of the World Cup see Eamon Dunphy – footballer-turned-broadcaster, author, controversialist – become the most reviled figure in Irish public life, again.

It is a role Dunphy knows from experience. He was one of the most consistent critics of Jack Charlton's tenure. As a panellist on RTÉ for our woeful 0–0 draw with Egypt in Italia 1990, he famously threw a pencil in disgust onto the desk and declared himself ashamed to be Irish. Days later he gatecrashed a press conference in Palermo and Jack refused to answer questions from someone he considered to be a) not a journalist, and b) 'a bitter little man'. When Dunphy refused to leave the room, Jack did. For a few minutes it was front-page news to the Italians.

'A boil on the arse of Irish soccer,' Dunphy once called Jack's successor, Mick McCarthy. A different article referred to a 'scurvy little pup'. McCarthy's friend and ghost, Cathal Dervan, recognised himself in the description and issued a legal writ. A settlement was reached after a three-day court hearing in May 1999. One of the prosecution's character witnesses was the Irish manager, Mick

McCarthy. Apart from the mutual baggage Keane and McCarthy carried to Korea/Japan, it was difficult to ignore the history of animosity shared by their respective Boswells. I have always liked Dunphy. Such was the level of gratitude during the Charlton era that there were times when you wondered if it had become illegal to ask awkward questions. Amid all the flag-waving, each of his hectoring invectives came as a blessing, like a cloudburst after months of sun. Irritating, inconsistent, and often infuriating, Dunphy has styled himself as the begrudger's begrudger, the worm in the fake rose of Irish football glory.

It was on his radio show, *The Last Word*, that the story first broke on the evening of Tuesday, 21 May. At the time it was around 3am in Saipan. Roy had turned in, adamant that he would be flying out at 4pm the next day. No statement had been issued by the FAI, nor had the manager held a press conference on the matter. Even to reporters actually on the island, the captain's imminent departure remained hearsay until a conclusive briefing by McCarthy at 9.30am on Wednesday morning. That Dunphy had the march on all the opposition, and was sufficiently confident of his sources to broadcast it on national radio, led to speculation about the extent of his contact with Roy. In his interview with Paul Kimmage, Roy denies any contact.

'Well, you know Eamon,' he says. 'But they would have had to book flights so it could have been a combination of anything.'

All that week Dunphy's appetite for a scrap remained insatiable. He clashed with the BBC's Ray Stubbs. He was, of course, in the Keane corner, up against Mark Lawrenson in Mick's.

'You would say that,' Stubbs goaded at one point, 'you're writing his biography.'

'That was a cheap shot,' Dunphy bit back.

He told a bemused Jeremy Paxman on BBC's *Newsnight* that Roy wanted to be part of an Irish team that aspired to being more than merely 'the cabaret act'. He clashed with John Bowman, presenter

and chairman of RTÉ's political debate programme, *Questions &
Answers*, on the night of Monday the 27th. Bowman, who would
have been far more comfortable fielding audience questions on the
formation of the new government, was clearly impatient with his
whole hour being given over to so trivial a subject. Dunphy's
cocktail of reason and rabble-rousing was getting under John's skin.

'So everyone's out of step with our Roy,' Bowman sneered.

'Talk about him with some respect, please.'

While Dunphy's line was altogether predictable, the manner of
its expression was seldom dull. The galaxy of quotes attributed to
him, in an ocean of flat platitudes, lit that week like flares fired up
from a drifting raft. Of Keane's criticisms of the FAI and expulsion
from the squad he said, 'This is not a case of someone who has been
caught with a lap dancer. This is the case of a man who has spoken
and earned the right to speak.' Of Jack Charlton's criticisms of Roy
and Paul McGrath on *The Late Late Show*, he wrote in *Ireland on
Sunday*: 'How dare this large, belligerent bloody-minded English
toe-rag cast aspersions on two magnificent men.' Asked to justify his
pro-Cameroon stance, he replied, 'I'm not a flag-waving lepre-
chaun out on the streets.'

One report even suggested that it was Dunphy to whom Michael
Kennedy turned as a final throw of the dice in the late afternoon of
Tuesday the 28th. Alex Ferguson had just tried persuading Roy to
apologise and had gotten nowhere. At 4pm Kennedy called
Dunphy and asked him to have a go. Dunphy and Roy discussed
at length the various factors involved in his decision: fitness, Roy's
relationship with the other members of the Irish squad, the likely
apportioning of blame if and when the results went pear-shaped.
'Can you bring yourself to apologise to McCarthy?' Dunphy asked.
'I can't,' Roy said. Dunphy told Roy to mull it over and called again
shortly before he went on air at five. Roy had made up his mind.

It was downhill from there. Dunphy continued to man his post
when it seemed anyone else qualified to comment had long since

deserted to the other camp. In the early hours of Saturday, 1 June, he appeared as a studio panellist for RTÉ's coverage of Ireland's opening match against Cameroon. He incensed the nation's viewers by expressing his hope that Cameroon would win and by wearing a tie in the colours of the Cameroon strip. By close of play that evening, RTÉ had fielded 1,300 complaints. He phoned in sick the next morning, when he was supposed to do the honours for England and Sweden. The complaints kept rolling in to the RTÉ switch. By Monday afternoon, when he spoke to a popular radio show, the total had crossed 2,000, the highest on any issue in the national broadcaster's history. A spokesman estimated that calls in his favour had not exceeded five and Dunphy joked, 'Even the Boston Strangler would have got a hundred!'

In spite of huge public pressure, RTÉ retained his services for coverage of the Germany game. As if conscious of the need to make conciliatory noises, he slagged off the opposition and praised Ireland's courage and resolve. His Road to Damascus came at half-time when he placed a bet on the boys in green to come out with a 1–1 draw and collected €1,200. To conclude, however, he expressed his regret that our best team wasn't on the field and that it had been a 'rubbish match'. It had, but we had reached the point where nobody was allowed to say so.

RTÉ retained his services up until and including coverage of hosts Japan against Russia, on the morning of Sunday, 9 June. He was visibly slurring his criticisms and had vanished by the half-time ads. By all accounts, the panellist had partaken of a few glasses of wine the night before, and arrived at the studio 'tired and emotional'. He apologised unreservedly. RTÉ finally took action, under intense public pressure and against the better judgement of the ratings analysis, suspending him for coverage of Ireland's final group game against Saudi Arabia that Tuesday, 11 June. According to its statement, Dunphy was 'unable to fulfil the terms of his contract'.

The last sighting of Roy's ghost during the weeks of Ireland's involvement in the World Cup was at a public screening of the Saudi Arabia game on 11 June. He was one of several guest panellists invited to discuss the match in front of over a thousand fans. Ironically, the event had been co-ordinated by the FAI. Before coverage began he was heckled for expressing his ongoing support of his friend, and after the match he brought the house down when he predicted that we would put up a strong fight against Spain five days later.

'I really wish we had our best team going out to play on Sunday,' he said.

Challenged by other guest panellists with the then widespread belief that the Irish team was stronger and more united after Keane's departure than it had been prior to it, he refused to accept what he clearly didn't believe to be true. Interrupted by ironic cheers and the odd chorus of 'loser', his words read like those of the last apostle of some old discredited belief system, preaching to heretics. Questioned afterwards on the stalemate of his relationship with RTÉ, and on the possibility of a comeback for the second-round clash with Spain, he told reporters, 'On Sunday I'll be sitting at home watching the match with maybe a few glasses of wine.'

41

The morning after the Saudi game Tommy gets into a dust at school. Since mid-May he has been collecting World Cup stickers for an album, and taking spares in to swap. Since the publishers were not sufficiently clairvoyant to foresee what would come to pass in Saipan, Roy still takes pride of place in the Ireland pages. He is 'inspirational' and 'uncompromising'. While the stats of most of his team-mates have inched forward fractionally since the album came out, his remain stranded as they were. You can get four different shots of him, and Tommy has every one several times over. A fortnight ago they were solid gold, now he can't give them away. Once or twice a week he transfers a euro from his piggybank into the zip pocket on the sleeve of his jacket and asks me to drive him uptown. He opens the packet there and then.

Initially, he was delighted for his own sake. He couldn't believe his luck, holding up the pack with a triumphant 'yes!' He was the first in his class to have all his Roy spaces filled. Anything after that was priceless for trading. Then the captain fell from grace, but Tommy's Roys kept coming. For a while he was delighted for his old man's sake. He said nothing, smiled manfully and showed them to me. I would make a point of exaggerating my own delight for the benefit of other customers, telling my son in a loud truculent voice how fortunate he was to have the best player ever to play for Ireland.

In the shelter at break on Wednesday, 5 June he offers a boy from the sixth class two Roys for one Del Piero. The boy, who supports Man United, says Roy is a tinker and I am called in to talk with the teacher after the final bell. I still don't know what happened, but what can I expect? For ten days he has heard his old man and gone in parroting the case for the defence. Now those second-hand opinions, probably rattled off word for word, are isolating him from his friends. He is confused. He knows we support Liverpool but like Roy, even though Roy plays for our sworn enemies. A bit bruised, he asks me, 'Why?'

'Why what?'

'Why do we like Roy?'

'Because he's Irish.'

'But there's loads of other Irish players who play for other clubs and you never go on about them.'

'Roy's special.'

'Why?'

'Because he's the Irish captain.'

'Used to be the Irish captain.'

'Used to be the Irish captain.'

'Does that mean we don't have to like him any more?'

42

Roy Keane is history now.

Mick McCarthy, *Ireland on Sunday*, 26 May 2002

Tim Murphy, his manager at Rockmount Boys, christened him 'The Boiler Man'. To Murphy he was 'the fellow who mans the furnace, who gets things heated up and keeps them that way'. When he stripped off at Anfield for his first league game most of the other players didn't even know his name. He told one reporter afterwards, 'We actually got on the pitch and the other Forest players were coming up and saying, "What's your name?"' Brian Clough hadn't the foggiest what to call him. Throughout his first season at the City Ground he remained Clough's 'young Irishman with the lovely smile'. The manager actually addressed him as 'Irishman'. It is now grist to the creation myth of Roy that Clough, in the Anfield dressing room, saw him helping the kitman and asked, 'Irishman, what are you playing at? Put that number seven shirt on.' In one game Forest were so stretched at the back that he was made a stand-in centre-half and Clough was moved to liken his performance to Franz Beckenbauer. For weeks his team-mates called him 'The Kaiser' and addressed him in comic-strip *Gott-in-Himmel* German accents.

'I wanted us to be anonymous,' Mick said of the choice of Saipan. Within a week his captain had become unmentionable. A prophetic reference to him was edited from the script of *Fair City*, RTÉ's inner-city soap opera, for the episode of Friday, 24 May: 'Ah sure, we'll be okay as long as Roy Keane doesn't lose the head.' 'Rage makes him great,' wrote Simon Barnes in *The Times*, 'and rage makes him unspeakable.' Some writers have taken that too literally. Big Jack referred to 'a certain young man . . . a disgrace to his country' in the *Irish Mirror*. A massive banner at the Cameroon game read 'Roy Who?' Philip Quinn wrote in the *Irish Independent* about 'the absence of you-know-who'. At the press conference after the Germany game one gormless American reporter asked about 'you-know-who'. The players shrugged and gazed at the floor until another question was raised. To a similar line of inquiry on a different occasion, Jason McAteer replied,

'Who? Oh him, yeah, yeah. I'd forgotten completely.'

The argument with the guy behind the meat counter in the supermarket was triggered by an official squad picture Sellotaped to the fridge door. One of the staff had blanked out Roy's face with a little luminous green sticker that read 'Reduced!' Next in line, I saw that, turned to catch the butcher's assistant smirking at me and lost it. It is like the picture from a Dublin building site that has appeared in all the papers. Roy's face has been cut out of the giant 7UP ad hung over scaffolding and three hard-hatted labourers are peering through. The street traders in town last Thursday were trying to flog their cheapo Keano T-shirts even cheaper. According to several reports, thousands of posters in Ireland's base in Chiba were scrapped and his body, but for a disembodied hand on the shoulder of the mascot, was successfully airbrushed from the group shot on the back of the team coach.

Some of the weekend papers have been revisiting old encounters between us and Spain as a preview to the game on Sunday. Miraculously, all mentions of the World Cup qualifier in Seville in November 1992 manage to overlook the man-of-the-match. They all remember that it was 0–0, that John Aldridge had a perfectly good goal disallowed for offside and that one of the Spaniards was sent for an early bath. But nobody, it seems, recalls the 21-year-old who patrolled the centre circle as if it were his own private island, nor the fact that Maradona was in the stand that night and swooned afterwards, 'Magnificent. Nobody could touch him. He is for the future.'

43

Tommy: 'Who do you think will take our penalties?'

Me: 'No idea.'

My Wife: 'It's very exciting, isn't it?'

Me: 'Very.'

Tommy: 'Dad, who do you think should take our penalties?'

Me: 'Oh, Keane, Duffer, Niall . . .'

Eve: 'My green gel pen is wasted.'

Tommy: 'Will Staunton take one?'

Me: 'No.'

Eve: 'Steve Staunton's a donkey. Daddy said so.'

My Wife (*laughing*): 'Leave your dad alone.'

Tommy: 'Dad . . .'

Me: 'What?'

Tommy: 'Will Staunton take a penalty?'

Me: 'NO!'

Tommy: 'Why not?'

Eve: 'The capital of Spain is Madrid.'

Me: 'Ah here.'

Tommy: 'Why not, Dad?'

Me: 'Because he was substituted before the end, and only the players still playing at the end of the game are allowed to take a penalty.'

My Wife: 'Do we have time for ice cream?'

Tommy: 'And what happens if we're the same score after the five penalties?'

Me: 'Then both teams take a sixth penalty. It's called sudden death.'

Eve: 'My friend's granny died.'

Tommy: 'And what happens if they both score, or if they both miss the sixth penalty?'

Me (*impatiently*): 'What do you think happens?'

Eve (*laughing*): 'They go for a cup of tea.'

Tommy (*laughing*): 'They take another one?'

Me: 'And another one, and another one, and another one, until one team misses and the other scores.'

Tommy: 'But what if we're the same score after everyone who was still playing at the end of the game has taken their penalties?'

Me: 'Go and get your ice cream before it gets cold.'

Eve: 'You mean, "before it gets warm and melts".'

Me (*sarcastically*): 'Thank you. Before it gets warm and melts.'

Tommy: 'Dad . . .'

Me: 'Never happens.'

Tommy: 'But it could though, couldn't it?'

Me: 'It could, but it won't.'

Tommy (*triumphantly*): 'But it could.'

Me: 'Yes, I suppose it could.'

Tommy: 'What would happen then?'

Eve (*eating ice cream and laughing*): 'They'd all go and buy ninety-nines.'

Tommy (*laughing*): 'Dad, what would happen then?'

Me: 'Don't know.'

Tommy: 'Would all the subs take one?'

Me: 'Uh-huh.'

Tommy: 'Would they, really?'

Me (*even more impatiently*): '*Yes.*'

Tommy: 'And what would happen if all the subs scored?'

Me: 'Ah Christ!'

My Wife (*eating ice cream and suddenly interested*): 'What *would* happen?'

Tommy: 'Would Mick McCarthy have to take one?'

Me: 'Yep.'

My Wife: '*Would* he?'

Me: 'Absolutely.'

Eve: 'And the man with the smelly armpits?'

Me: 'Camacho? Absolutely.'

Tommy: '*Really*?'

My Wife: 'And if all the managers scored, then the fans would have a go.'

Tommy: 'Would they, Dad?'

Me: 'Absolutely. Keep yourself warmed up in case they come to you.'

Tommy (*jumping on one spot*): 'Oh God.'

My Wife: 'Looks like we're about to start.'

Eve: 'There's a woman in Russia and she has X-ray eyes.'

Tommy: 'Robbie Keane's going first. Do you think we'll win, Dad?'

The afternoon of 16 June, 2002, a Sunday. We have just watched another heroic 1–1 win, this time against Spain in the World Cup second round. They took the lead after eight minutes, missed a few chances; we got two penalties from the Danish ref, missed the first and scored the second in injury time. In future, if and when Ireland reaches the knockout stages of major finals, it might be worth the FAI's while proposing that we just go straight to penalties.

I was full sure that Mick's jar of jam would run dry, but for the fourth time in three weeks couldn't say as much. There were, admittedly, waves of instinctive pride at the sight of Damien Duff, a ragamuffin from Rathfarnham, treating household Spanish names like slalom poles. And there were, by necessity, the tried-and-trusted blurts of support, especially when it seemed we were looking down the barrel at defeat. Today my bluff as an Irish fan seemed to fool even my wife. 'Don't give up, don't give up,' she said as if her husband were on the brink of giving birth. Even the gods had the wool pulled over their eyes. Twice I shouted 'Penalty!' and twice my prayers were answered. Next time I keep my big mouth shut.

Just as the penalties are about to commence, it all gets too much. I excuse myself on the pretence of a routine call of nature, silently put the door on the snib and am at the end of the close before I know it. It is only a two-minute step from our house to the town's main drag. A short, distant roar. Robbie must have scored. Then a lull in which either one of their guys is taking his time or has scored too.

During Italia 1990 reports of all Ireland's matches on the national news featured footage of the streets of our major cities while play was in progress. Dublin, Cork, Galway were ghost towns. Grafton Street looked the way it looks on Christmas Day. They were beautiful shots, a bit like listening to the muffled dialogue and laughter of a play from directly behind the stage. Italia 1990 was our first World Cup. It was as if the country, infatuated with its new-found success, was happy to gaze starstruck at itself from all angles like some adolescent Adonis with a handful of mirrors in the bathroom on a summer afternoon. Korea/Japan is our third and the newsrooms haven't gone to so much trouble this time around.

The lull drags on. The main shopping streets are completely deserted, except for yours truly and one old codger with a cocker spaniel who says in passing, 'You're as bad as me.' He must think I'm pacing the pavements because I can't bear the prospect of Ireland losing. A second, less concerted roar. The security alarms of several shops are warbling like songbirds in April. A third, slightly longer roar. An ambulance goes past at breakneck speed, violet strobe rotating and sirens silent. This time twelve years ago in Dublin, it was common to see fire engines and squad cars blaring through the streets minutes before the kick-off of one of our games. The joke at bus stops was, 'She's got the kettle on.' The ambulance gets to the island at the junction of the two biggest streets and careers left through a still red light. This is more serious. It starts to whoop the second it disappears out of sight. After that there are no more roars.

I feel guilty. I have willed Ireland to lose and for the rest of the day the fact that they have lost will seem like more than a coincidence. The skyline is littered with sirens and barking. It's like the all-clear after a nuclear alert. The punters start to trickle out onto the pavement, bleary-eyed and glad still to be in one piece. Mostly women and girls at first, decked out in Ireland jerseys and bandanas, some singing 'Olé, Olé, Olé, Olé' as a last gesture of pride. One guy, pissing against the shutter of Lifestyle Sports, cranes back and grins my way in consolation, 'Don't take it too hard, sunshine.'

Tommy meets me in the hall.

'What happened you?'

'Sorry.'

'We lost.'

'I guessed.'

'Did you see it?'

'No. I just heard people talking.'

'Bloody Matt Holland and Kevin Kilbane and David Connolly should be shot.'

'Ah Tom. Were they the ones who missed?'

'Evie could've done better.'

It is also Bloomsday. It is also Father's Day. Neither of which means much to me or my family. Except that when my wife and me spent a summer working in Norway in 1993 we had only one book between us: *Ulysses*. We read it separately at least three times and by September were quizzing one another with obscure Blazes Boylan trivia. We have marked 16 June ever since by each finding a single stinker with which to stump the other. This year we don't bother. Except that my kids insist on giving me presents. My wife buys and wraps them. After tea Eve gives me a black Boss sweater, and Tommy a copy of Eamon Dunphy's memoir of the 1973/4 season with Millwall, *Only a Game?*

44

There have been a couple of questions hanging in the air since last Sunday, although nobody has asked them. Would Roy have taken a penalty? Would Roy have scored? He would probably have been obliged because of his seniority in the team and the weight has proven too great for great players: Platini, Pearce, Baggio. A Keano balloon over the bar in Suwon would have been hard to bear.

I know of only three penalties taken by Keane in his club career. The first was for Forest in 1990, in the final of a pre-season reserves tournament in Haarlem, Holland. All the penalty shoot-outs of Italia 1990 were still fresh in their heads, especially for apprentices of a club whose first-team captain had missed in the semis against West Germany. Keane went fifth and last, and was mobbed by his team-mates when the ball hit the net. The second was in the shoot-out to decide the Charity Shield in August 1997. He scored that one too and did his cruciate six weeks later.

When he stepped up to take that last penalty, he possibly had in his mind another one missed for Ireland earlier the same year against Romania, 30 April 1997. It was a qualifier for France 1998, on in the background during a joint birthday party for Tommy and Eve. My extended family had come down for grub and wine. We had trailed by a single Adrian Ilie volley from the first half. Then, just as the cake was being lined with candles, Ray Houghton got his ankles rapped by the keeper and the ref waved towards the spot. John Aldridge, the regular penalty taker, wasn't there. Ray himself didn't fancy it, nor did the captain Andy Townsend fancy it. Even I muttered quizzically, '*Roy Keane?*' It was weak, knee-high, and only slightly to the keeper's right. I still don't remember my exact words, only that the joint birthday party broke up much earlier than scheduled and I spent the next week apologising to my wife and my mother.

All diehards harbour memories they think no one else shares. You are certain otherwise meaningless games survive only in your head because of their significance in your life. I thought that about Sophia 1997. Then variations of 'missed penalty against Romania in World Cup qualifier' appeared in almost every career rundown that the papers ran immediately after Saipan. The country had still not forgiven him. The one interesting exception appeared in the *Daily Mirror* on 24 May. It was a photo of Roy's penalty from behind the goal. The keeper has just palmed the ball away, and Roy is standing aghast in the background. Its wistfully erroneous caption reads:

> A cool Roy Keane leads by example as he dispatches a well-hit penalty past Romanian goalkeeper Bogdan Stelea.

45

On the morning of 18 June, the following Tuesday, the squad touches down in Dublin. They are put up once more in the Holiday Inn on the roundabout at the entrance to Dublin Airport. They shower and change into their official suits for an audience with the President that afternoon. David Connolly's hasn't arrived, and Dean Kiely has to cadge the chef's. Bertie Ahern is also at the reception. Afterwards the squad is led to an open-air party with 100,000 fans. Mick tells them they are wonderful. They cheer.

They cheer as Mick introduces the team one by one and each wanders across the stage waving. The players are then interviewed. It is relayed live on RTÉ television and radio. I have it on in the background while packing for France, the volume muted. They look at sea in their suits, like debutantes practising open-mouthed kisses. Every word Jason utters is uproarious. Westlife perform in suits that are white with one orange sleeve and one green. Mick has been given a new two-year contract. The FAI's office has received, in a giant envelope, 300 letters and poems by the kids of a Dublin national school. A seat in a theatre in Athlone, with the names of all the squad (bar one) engraved on it, has been paid for on their behalf by a grateful patron. Someday I hope to sit on it.

Two evenings later we have a bon voyage dinner up in my mother's house. We can hear, from behind the row of houses directly opposite, the music of the street party convened for the returning hero. Much to my mother's horror, I express more than once my wish that the heavens open. The guest of honour, according to subsequent reports in the regional rags, accepts a piece of local crystal in the shape of a football and says a few well-chosen words into the ad hoc PA.

I have never understood the law of nature whereby one is obliged to be unquestioningly proud of another's achievements simply because that other happens to hail from a few grim streets away. Three weeks listening to his name being put forward as a paragon of tact and decency have taken their toll. Fuelled by my mother's obvious unease and a surplus of Shiraz, I slide open the door into the front garden and, to my eternal shame, roar at full tilt, 'Staunton!'

'I'll ask you politely,' my mother is saying, 'to please come in. These are my neighbours.'

'Staunton, you fucking yes-man!'

At lunchtime next day, the summer solstice, Staunton goes to meet the pupils of our old school just down the road. He is met and hugged by the present principal. In subsequent pics he looks as if it had been a late night and she is wearing a velvet Ireland hat in the shape of a Viking helmet. On the front wall is chalked: STEVEN STAUNTON OUR MOST FAMOUS PUPIL. The *Argus*, Dundalk's biggest-selling weekly, reads much into the fact that he comes alone:

This was not a stage-managed moment, there were no PR gurus, no minders and no fanfare, the Irish captain drove himself in the school gates and ambled down to the infants' schoolyard.

That afternoon I meet a different reporter on the way in to the opening of a public art show in the local college. She asks if I am going to the civic reception in the square tonight.

'No,' I say.

She peers at me, all amused incredulity.

'One hundred and two international caps,' she says. 'You can't argue with that.'

'No,' I sniff. 'It seems you can't.'

As it happens, the heavens do open in the square that evening. It rains so hard that a postponement is seriously considered. On the trailer of a lorry he hears speeches from various dignitaries. He is presented with a scroll on behalf of the town council. To a meadow of golf umbrellas he jokes that he brought home the monsoon season if not the World Cup and a cheer fills the gap where laughter is meant to be. His legendary left peg sprays ten signed balls into the crowd. Audience questions are put to him via the MC. Yes, he would have taken a penalty. He was christened 'Stan' by his first Liverpool team-mates in memory of an old pro with Chester. An autograph queue is formed to a backdrop of thunder and forked lightning that crackles like the devil's ire.

Mentions of the devil are cool and far between. There was, he suggests, a lot that went on behind the scenes. It just wasn't to be. According to the *Dundalk Democrat*, the devil's name had been uttered in council chambers last Monday. The county councillors accepted a vote of congratulation to the Irish team. There then ensued a light-hearted debate as to which of the county's main towns, Drogheda (where he was born) or Dundalk (where he grew up), could claim Ireland's World Cup captain. The hilarity was truncated and any other business quickly addressed when one councillor 'spoiled it all by mentioning the Corkman'.

PART II

Extra Time

I was on holidays in Portugal over the summer and I
saw Stan across the square in this little village. I
wanted to go and talk to him. I should have done. I
would have to have told him I thought he was
wrong to do the press conference. He would have
told me the same probably. I'd have said that I
understood where he was coming from but I
wouldn't have done it, that if Mick had asked him to
jump in the river he would have done that too. But
I was with my wife and kids and he was with his
wife and kids. It was best not to start into it all.

Roy Keane, *Irish Times*, 31 August 2002

46

My own footballing past, such that it is, has the banal tragedy of most footballing pasts. The town we grew up in, at the time when we were of an age to join teams, had the most successful club in the League of Ireland. We sold programmes in front of the stand, and in return we got free crisps and admittance. There were league and cup doubles, and a few famous nights in Europe. The PSV Eindhoven team that had the van de Kerkhof twins played here. We drew 1–1 at home with Spurs in the Cup Winners Cup, and lost 1–0 away. We got stuffed 4–1 by Liverpool in 1982 in the European Cup.

We lost 3–2 on aggregate to Celtic in the same tournament in a different year. Twenty-two thousand fans packed into the home leg. The club had the brainwave of spilling heaps of gravel beside the pitch and shaping them like terraces. It was like trying to watch a football match from the Sahara Desert. The night before the game my grandfather, who lived in Glasgow until his own father was killed in a gas explosion, put on his Celtic tie and linked my mother up the road to watch them train. He was eighty-one. For most of the session he complained that he couldn't see beyond the green wall. It was the pitch. They got talking to a bunch of travelling fans outside the ground.

'I spent the first twelve years of my life in the shadow of Park Head,' my grandfather told them.

'Is tha' right, Jimmy?'

After they got back, he asked my mother, 'How did that chap know my name?'

So we wanted to be footballers. We joined a club based in a field called The Clump not far from where we lived: Casement Celtic

FC. We were managed by a milkman, Jackie Henry, who ferried us to and from matches in the open back of his van. Our strip was orange top and blue shorts, a bit like Brazil gone wrong in the wash. Not that the colours meant much to the plump ten-year-old who watched almost all games from the touchline in his anorak. After the first match of my first season Jackie said, 'It'll be your turn next week, son.' Jackie, I'm still waiting for the nod to strip off.

That's not entirely fair. Jackie had twelve lads. Even chubbier and worse than me was Ollie. Ollie's dad had a chain of hotels, sponsored the kit and was ringside at every kick-off with a sheepskin jacket and a half corona. There was grumbling in the ranks when the team sheet on which Ollie's was the last name got called out, but what could Jackie do?

It's not entirely true either. Although it took more than a full season, I did eventually get a game and a bit. The bit came first. One of our central midfielders twisted his ankle and couldn't shake it off. Jackie left it as long as he could before giving me my cue. He had forgotten my name. The guy hobbled off. I trundled on. I was on for all of seven or eight minutes, marvelling at the muddy ball bobbling around. Then Jackie drew the ref's attention to a second substitution; only I knew we didn't have any other subs. I remember seeing him calling me over, the other guy hobbling back on, and me taking an age to compose myself and ask, 'Can you do that?'

The full game came in a cancelled cup-tie. We had only ten, so the coach of the other team sportingly agreed to play it as a friendly. I was right wing and did okay. Jackie even said so at half-time. It finished 1–1. We led for so long that Jackie had begun to make noises about this being the tie proper. You could hear the raised voices of both managers on the touchline. Then they got the equaliser in the dying moments and, cup or friendly, we had to play again. I had the last touch of the game. It came straight from the restart and I was tripped. I rolled around on the grass, theatrically, assuming the blown whistle had been for a free. It was for full time. When I opened my eyes, most of our players and theirs had trudged off, and I was sprawled on the pitch on my own.

I got picked for the school team the following year. I started the first game at centre forward. I was taken off at half-time and the teacher in charge gave me his anorak. I didn't play again. Not only did I not get another game, I wasn't even required to tog out. Our old man's favourite gag at the time was that his second youngest wasn't so much 'an outside left' as 'a left outside'.

I went around to training at 'The Clump' for a few more summers, to punctuate the boredom if nothing else. Still, even to this day, whenever I go for a kickabout with Tommy, I can hear Jackie roaring, 'Get your hands out of your pockets.' The day after the Germany game, I remembered a bollocking Jackie gave us one evening at training. That each of us, age-wise, was still in single digits cut no ice with Jackie. We lacked commitment, the killer instinct.

'Look at Steven Staunton,' he kept yelling.

There had been talk of some kid who lived in one of the houses around The Clump, but who played for a different club. Already he was being tipped to go far.

'Look at young Staunton. *He* has commitment. *He* has the killer instinct. He never goes anywhere without a football.'

47

We see the World Cup final in France. We are there for a month. Tommy and me keep our Brazil T-shirts clean for the weekend of the match. Why does everyone support Brazil every World Cup? It makes no sense. It's all part of a carefully marketed illusion that they play the beautiful game with all the freedom of teenagers in bare feet on a beach, supported by tanned girls dancing the samba. It is also nostalgia for something that those of us who can't remember 1970 heard of from our fathers, for that afternoon during España 1982 when we blubbed and swore to watch neither the semis nor the final, and for the boredom all those Junes spent attempting to bend a ball into the top corner of an open garage door. These days Brazil samba only when the job is done, and getting the job done can be a struggle. The phenomenon is summed up by the waitress of a pizzeria we eat at the Saturday evening before the final. She is wearing canary yellow as well. Half out of chaste flirtation and half to give my pretty stilted French an airing, I ask, 'Vous êtes Brésilienne?'

'Non,' she laughs, 'j'aime les couleurs.'

The whole of the Languedoc likes the colours. We're crossing the parking lot on the way back from the supermarket with stuff for Sunday lunch, when a local kid notices our tops and bellows rhetorically from the shade of a palm tree, 'Brésil à gagner!'

I think he means 'Brazil to win', or something like that.

'Oui.'

'Oui,' an old madame passing at the same time utters with much more passion than yours truly. 'J'espère, j'espère . . .'

It occurs to us that there must be any number of old folks still around who remember the occupation by German troops too clearly to pretend to be neutral. The *centre ville* falls silent during the match. We watch it on the roof terrace, with baguettes and coffee and the telly draped in a beach towel. When Ronaldo scores just after the restart, a dull roar of relief rises up from the shuttered murk of a thousand living rooms. Compared to them, our support of Brazil is a shallow thing. Ronaldo scores again and the second longer roar is borne more out of bitter nose-rubbing than relief. Jesus, we're thinking, they really mean this. The only man in the South of France on Rudi Völler's side is Tommy. It has just dawned on him that Germany are the kids' syndicate's top seed in the family buster, and his nibs blubs a bit at the thought of €80 going down the drain. Eve stands to lose the same and doesn't bat an eyelid. We promise ice cream (*deux boules*) after the tickertape presentation, on the condition that my son keeps his Brazil shirt on and his allegiance to himself.

One night over coffee down in 'Le Commerce', while our kids are playing among the trees, my wife and me get to talking about how Irish we feel, or what being Irish does and doesn't mean to us. In any calendar year there are hundreds of academic conferences worldwide that gravitate back to this. To our educated generation it's considered just about the corniest question you could ask, one likely to clear a room quicker than a shout of 'Fire!' So much so, however, that we haven't once discussed it in thirteen years together. Just like that, I ask her, 'So how Irish do you feel?'

'Oh God! I've never thought a thing about it.'

Now that we mention it, we agree we feel more Irish abroad than at home. We are seldom slow to make our country of origin obvious. We enjoy the benign goodwill with which Irishness is welcomed. In France, for example, Tommy establishes our exotic national credentials with his tricolour beach towel. He unfurls it on the hot sand, puts on his togs and walks to the water with his seven-year-old don't-mess-with-me swagger amid odd murmurs of 'Ah, Irlandais!'

We even like other Irish people abroad. On the autoroute down we overtook a car with a Cork reg and exchanged flashed headlights and beeped horns. We eavesdrop on familiar accents at market stalls and ask them where they're from. Stranger still, we feel closer to English people than when we're at home. It can't be just the language, since that affinity doesn't kick in with Yanks and Aussies. Our landlord and his good lady, who moved over from Ipswich a few years ago, have taken to sitting at our table odd mornings in a way they say they don't usually do. They pass on football news, rumours from the summer transfer market, and we all gloat about the shit weather 'at home'.

It is glaringly obvious where I am coming from on all this, and my wife strings me along. Almost all the website entries from emigrants during the World Cup came down on Roy like a tonne of bricks. It was odd reading words like 'deserter' and 'traitor' written by Irish men and woman as far flung as San Diego and Singapore. Perhaps where you come from means more when you're not there. When you live abroad home becomes a kind of safety net elsewhere, and your days are underwritten by the precious insurance policy that is your national identity. When you live in Ireland you think about Irishness as much and in much the same terms as you think about, say, one of those Baileys gift sets they sell on special offer at the checkouts in Duty Free: that is, almost never and then only as something sickly sweet that's manufactured exclusively for the export market.

We visit English friends in the Cévennes. Their son tells us about watching the last minutes of the Ireland–Germany game in a sports store in Nîmes. He says all the staff and customers gathered beneath one of the monitors, and the whole place went berserk when Robbie Keane scored in the ninety-second minute.

48

About a month before Korea/Japan, I get commissioned to review a couple of footie books for the *Irish Times*. This is a first and I am chuffed. Too chuffed. I get carried away and, when filing, include a biog note that says the reviewer 'once played on the same team as Steve Staunton'. Suddenly, emails start flooding in from friends I haven't heard from for ages, and every cat and dog in the town is telling me, 'Loved your biog note in the paper . . .'

I laugh along at first, but after a week or two it grates. I want to ask them about the article, but keep my manners. It's a bit like doing a poetry reading. Someone is bound to come up every time and say, 'Loved your intros.'

'Thanks a million.'

The Staunton afterthought is completely true. But it has come to be viewed as one of those scraps of apocrypha, retold with a slight inflection in the voice, as if it carries an implied asterisk and a footnote underlining its uncertain origins. I was approached to play in the summer street league for an under-eleven team based nearby. My next eldest brother acted as go-between. The deal was struck one morning while I was walking to school. A car pulled alongside me. It was the coach and his two sons, one of whom was in the team. I remember sitting in mortified silence, the two sons staring at me and the man seeming unsure if it was yes or no.

This was Gaelic football, that uniquely Irish halfway house between soccer and Aussie Rules. The season was already under way and I started without attending a single practice session. I played at the centre of defence. Rocket science it wasn't. I had to catch high balls and pump them, hard and fast, from whence they came. We must have been doing okay. We came runners-up. But I was lost in a fog of my own making and don't remember noticing much else about the games other than what I did.

Staunton was star man. He was plain old Steven in those days. He was a year younger than me. Usually, at that age, someone a year your junior seems like a kid, as someone a year your senior seems ancient. But his presence on the pitch, and that demeanour of shouldering the weight of the world he would never lose, demanded we grudgingly look up to him. He was playmaker and goal scorer all in one. Before the kick-off and the restart the coach talked tactics with Steven. The only tactical advice the rest of us were given was: 'Get the ball to Steven.'

The last game of the season was a showdown against the team that eventually came first. I must have been unusually spaced out, even by the standards of your average ten-year-old boy. I had no idea this was the crunch tie until one of the fathers said as much at half-time. We went to pieces after that. I started missing the high balls, and so did most of the others. Late in the game, when it was past saving, I was trying to clear our lines. I had an acre of time and space, but couldn't get the ball out from under my feet. Steven ran the length of the pitch to dispossess me, hissing a sarcastic, 'Good man. Well played.'

The following two Tuesday evenings I trundled around as usual to the wall outside the coach's house, where the team waited to be collected for a game. The first time I sat there a good hour. Nobody came and I went home. It didn't occur to me to ring the doorbell. A week later the coach's son came out, considered me quizzically for a minute, then said, 'The season's over.'

He went back inside. That last bit never became part of the story, until now.

I played on the same side as Steven in the annual match in our primary school between the two senior classes. This was possibly that summer, or perhaps the following, but certainly no later. We were in the same year in different classes at the same school. I was under a profoundly violent GAA-orientated foghorn who wilted and died after the abolition of corporal punishment. Steven was in the class of the gentler, more literate master who kept a cricket ball on his desk and got misty-eyed about Ireland's rugby greats.

It was my one moment of football glory. I had always been one of those lads who got left to last when it came to picking teams. So it was no shock when I was considered surplus to the requirements of our class's team and was granted a free transfer to the short-staffed opposition. I was put up front. (What is it about bad players and centre forward?) I got thick. Getting thick has always been my strongest sporting attribute. What I lacked in poise and pace I occasionally made up for with pigheadedness. This was one hu-militation too far.

I scored the game's only goal. It was early in the first half. The ball was wide on the left. I was near post, backing into one of their (*our*) defenders and called for it to be played into my feet. Is it writing it up a little too much to say the game stood still a split second after I called? I never usually called. I was one of those that hid silently behind their player standing between our player in possession and me. I was one of those who suffered butterflies when a pass was on the cards. This time I called 'Yes' and Steven skimmed one in, low and fast. I caught it, swivelled onto the left and buried it high into the net.

'Good goal, sonny.'

Our teacher was also referee. He called all of us 'sonny', menacingly. I didn't answer or meet his eye. I wasted the rest of the game waiting for the final whistle to run home and tell my brothers. We won. Or rather, *they* won and I got their goal. For an evening it felt as if I had been let go to Liverpool by United for a song, and had gone back to Old Trafford and scored the winner.

Somebody once said that, on the evidence of present claimants, there must have been about 20,000 paying punters at the Dandelion Market (admission 10p) to see the inchoate U2 in the late seventies. The team in which Steven Staunton played, in the town we both think of as home, has grown similarly over the years. I don't kid myself that Staunton remembers any of the above. The most I can hope for is that he won't mind my remembering it, nor the fact that my memory gains its modicum of glamour on the strength of his presence in it and his fame in the intervening years.

Shortly after that match, school broke for the summer. Then we went to different secondary schools. I have this vivid recollection from about five years later, of my mother buying petrol for an old Ford Escort automatic with no reverse gear. We borrowed it Monday–Friday from a friend of the family who worked in the civil service in Dublin during the week. She fed it two pounds and that saw us through the week. The petrol station owner, in the few seconds it took, was saying, 'I hear young Staunton has signed for Liverpool.'

49

Benny, my barber, has news. Since we've been gone David O'Leary has lost his job as manager of Leeds United and the FAI has sold the rights to all our matches to Sky. David will always have, as they say, a special place in the hearts of Irish football fans, thanks mainly to his winning penalty against Romania, Genoa, 1990. Those images – David walking to the box, Jack laughing bashfully at the irony of his immediate success depending upon one of the old guard he had banished to the bench, and Liam Brady shouting on ITV 'Just knock it in, David' – have become part of all our pasts. RTÉ has even broadcast a whole half-hour documentary around that one kick, in which both the Irish team's assistant physio Mick Byrne and *Father Ted* star Ardal O'Hanlon put forward the belief that the Celtic Tiger was born at that moment.

David had a four-minute meeting with his club chairman, Peter Risdale, on the last Thursday in June, after which he cleared his desk and drove home. Risdale initially said it was by mutual agreement, but later confirmed it had been a sacking. The official reason cited Leeds' bad season. However, it was reported in most places that the planned sale of Rio Ferdinand to Manchester United had become an issue. David wanted to keep Rio and Risdale said the club needed the money.

In the first week of July the FAI announced details of its new deal with Sky. Up until then all our home and away games had been shown for free within Ireland by the national broadcaster, and Sky had the rights for Britain. Now all our matches will be available only on satellite. Benny subscribes to Sky and yet is livid. It occurs to me as Benny speaks that the real issue is not so much that we have to pay for it, but that we are subsidising a foreign company for the privilege to view the boys in green. Benny views this the way most people view those anachronistic ground rents on Irish townhouses that still get paid to Home Counties peers. Righteous indignation does wonders for his grammar.

'How dare they,' he keeps repeating. 'How fuckin' dare they!'

He means the FAI, not Sky. The deal was announced a mere fortnight after the Phoenix Park reception. Just when it seemed they had emerged from the World Cup war as the good guys, the association has shot itself in the foot again. Now that he feels completely vindicated, Benny has no qualms revisiting the whole Saipan affair. He begins every second sentence with 'You see Keane's fatal error was . . .' I ham up my stereotypical begrudger. It has occurred to both of us how weird this is: two youngish Irishmen, one happy to shelter beneath the umbrella of 'we' and one standing out under the cloud of a neutral 'you'.

'Fifty-sixth to thirteenth in the world rankings in six years,' Benny says. 'You can't argue with that.'

'For five and a half of those six McCarthy was lucky enough to have the best midfielder in the world.'

'I just don't understand you Keane lads. The team performed absolutely magnificently without him, and still you're whingeing. Put up and shut up, that's what I say.'

'They were crap.'

'How can you say that? How can you say that?'

Another cul de sac. I veer off onto the David O'Leary secondary road. I remind Benny that Mick is 4–1 to get the job. He says nothing. I point out that Mick is from Yorkshire and list all the Irish players on Leeds' books: Gary Kelly, Stephen McPhail, Ian Harte . . .

'It would be just like coming home.'

Nothing. I can tell this angle of needling is getting through. The manager Benny and his ilk stuck by is suddenly prepared to drop it all and run.

'O'Leary could take over the Ireland job, and we'd all be one big family again.'

'*We* already have a manager, thank you very much.'

50

'We' is also Liverpool. Like most families in Ireland in the seventies, 'we' were Leeds. Not just because Leeds won almost everything, but also because the Irish captain, Johnny Giles, played for them. Almost everyone of my generation in Ireland has an old man who still supports Leeds. Sometimes you feel like saying to one of them, 'You do realise that Giles has retired, don't you?'

For a couple of years we floated, swayed by the random colours of the jerseys we got every Christmas. Our mother went down to a shop owned by one of the stars of the local club and returned with an armful of crestless acrylic jobs that were snagged on barbed wire before the third round of the FA Cup had been played. I got one that was amber with black lapels and cuffs, and for the latter half of that season and the first of the next my older brothers told me I supported Wolves. When the eldest got a green one with white trims he spent a year as Pat Jennings, the Arsenal keeper with hands like tennis rackets and an accent as thick as Newry fog. It never occurred to any of us that our brother could be Ireland. Then it happened. Someone got red with white trims, Johnny Giles defected to West Brom, Liverpool achieved what Leeds didn't by winning the European Cup, the rest of us asked for red as well the Christmas after that and our old man, in a moment of isolated pique, told us we were 'disloyal little friggers'.

In our defence, Liverpool had an Irish flavour. That felt good. It justified a certain red/green colour blindness. In my father's time, there was Steve Highway, the winger who looked like a dachshund. We made much of the fact that a solitary 'O' stood between our middle brother and the man who holds the record for club caps, Ian Callaghan. At different stages during Jack Charlton's decade at the helm, no fewer than nine Irish players passed through Liverpool's books. When left back Jim Beglin's career effectively ended in the Mersey derby in 1987, his position was filled by an eighteen-year-old from our hometown who would in turn take over as captain in Saipan.

Staunton was seventeen when he signed, so this would have been 1986. He left Steven. By the time he was a permanent fixture in the Liverpool first eleven, he had been reincarnated in the mouths of the commentators. The tacit collective embarrassment of 'Steve' was overcome by the fact that it was Liverpool. We had generally accepted that none of us was likely to tog out in Anfield in this life. A kid from town getting the nod instead was more than adequate compensation. When *Match of the Day* read out the team sheets before their featured games, you could almost feel the local power supply overheating.

His earliest outing in green that I remember was away to Spain in 1989, a qualifier for Italia 1990 and, in the old post-match parlance, a bloody nightmare. We lost 2–0 and several of the newspapers next morning sympathetically suggested that Steven (*Stan*) had much to learn. I received my first ever acceptance of poems from a magazine the same day. At the time I was living in Grosvenor Square on Dublin's south side. Me and my brother had a dreadful flat that was last redecorated in 1971, with a fridge in the sitting room where the telly should have been that we sat and looked at every night. My brother was a newly qualified accountant who was enjoying life on the dole too much to go job-hunting, and I was pretending to be a writer. The economic boom was a few years in the offing. One Wednesday night, nothing to do and still suffering pangs of homesickness at the age of twenty, I hitched back up to watch the match in comfort. There was an envelope with an English stamp waiting beside the telephone, addressed to me in my own hand.

For much of the intervening decade and a half I thought that appearance in Seville was Staunton's Irish debut. I told it in such a way as to suggest an uncanny parallel between two great careers. I have only bothered to check the veracity of the story in the past twenty minutes. Staunton togged out first for his country against Tunisia in October 1988. Spain was his second game. Nor do the parallels run like tramlines after that. I waited the guts of a year for the magazine to appear. Staunton was back in harness before the winter was out. I waited the guts of a year after publication for what poetry editors traditionally call 'a slim cheque': two pounds sterling. It is glued into a scrapbook somewhere in our attic, with a caption by me underneath: 'May their accounts be forever in shite!' Does Staunton's accountant have a corresponding tale? I doubt it.

In spite of Seville, Jack kept faith with Stan. He had a good attitude and a bit of talent. Jack's captain, Mick McCarthy, liked him too. There is one old yarn from the early days of Jack. The squad was together for some qualifying game. Staunton tiptoed into the dressing room and happened upon some of the senior players in the depths of a card school. Liam Brady, then one of the immortals of world football, without looking up said something like, 'Tea and biscuits, there's a good lad.'

Staunton went about his business. As he was leaving he muttered, 'Get your own fuckin' tea and biscuits.'

By the time we lined up against Bobby Robson's England in Cagliari, he had made the position of left back his own. In the footage of the moments immediately after our equaliser, Stan is the first at Sheedy's shoulder, grinning as if all his birthdays had come at once. Stan was the only Irish player to fire a shot in anger in the 0–0 nightmare that followed against Egypt. Stan was waiting in the centre spot when Dave O'Leary scored his penalty against Romania. Stan was the blond mullet on top of the double-decker that paraded from the airport into Dublin city centre.

51

One of the more bizarre sequels of the World Cup has been the new ad for Surf Automatic washing powder, featuring Mrs Niall Quinn. A couple of weeks ago my wife went along to a reception in Bowe's on Fleet Street, and got chatting with a woman who described her advertising firm's recent run-in with Lever Brothers.

For several years, up until this summer, ads for Surf have featured Mary McEvoy, formerly Biddy of *Glenroe*, the Irish equivalent of *Emmerdale*. Initially, Mary was on her lonesome, enunciating her catchphrase to camera. The ads graduated into mini dramas in which Mary was wooed by a goofy checkout boy in her local supermarket. But, while Lever Brothers was prepared to applaud the imagination of those ads, the bottom line was that super-annuated soap stars do not sell soap powder in sufficient units.

Now Surf is being sold to the nation's housewives by Gillian Quinn. She's perfect, as you might expect from the wife of a perfect gentleman. She has those girl-next-door looks that would prompt your average barrister into a laddish joke before teeing off in the captain's prize. Niall, conspicuous by his absence, is selling the product by proxy. At one point Gillian even takes a break from the laundry to look at a photo of her husband and children, as you do, lest we forget what a terrific family man he is. Gillian catches a jersey thrown from off camera and rolls her eyes in mock exasperation. It seems we are expected to believe that Niall drives home from Premier League matches in his muddy kit, comes bounding into the kitchen hollering, 'Gillian, I'm home love, we got a late equaliser, again . . .' and peels off there and then.

The final shot is a hoot. Gillian throws an unopened box of Surf back to 'Niall', unseen in the wings. We hear a grunt and a thud that signifies a drop. Gillian turns back towards us, shrugs coquettishly and says, 'Well, he's no goalkeeper!' We are expected to infer sex, albeit sex within the sanctity of marriage. Niall Quinn is present by his absence, and his wife Gillian is telling us what he is (a scorer) by telling us what he isn't. Surf has been selling like hot cakes ever since.

52

For some reason best known to himself, Stan wasn't one of the two Irish internationals on the pitch for our league game against Nottingham Forest, 28 August 1990. The match, a comfortable home win thanks to Messrs Rush and Beardsley, was unremarkable but for the league debut of a kid from Cork of whom nobody had ever heard. The kid clattered Whelan inside ten minutes and had an eyeballing session with Houghton. Myself and my new girlfriend were flat-hunting in Dublin that night. Dispirited, we went drinking and I asked the guy behind the bar if he'd heard the score of the Liverpool game. You can always tell if a barman is on your side or not. If he describes the goals in loving detail, then you know you have a mutual unspoken allegiance. This guy, I figure, was United. I was laughing at him and he knew it. We were still the aristocrats and United's manager, Alex Ferguson, was getting stick.

'Two-nil,' he said flatly and not once looking up from his *Evening Herald*.

'Thank you. Scorers?'

'Haven't a clue.'

'Gentleman.'

My earliest sighting was some time towards the end of 1990. My new girlfriend and I had just moved into a basement flat on St Alphonsus Road, Drumcondra. It took a few weeks for my dole to transfer to the north side of the Liffey, and when it did I splashed out on a year's subscription to cable TV with the arrears. I wanted to watch the Ashes test series live from Australia. But I also enjoyed the added bonus of *Match of the Day*. One Saturday night, not long in from The Gravediggers, I was semi-comatose on the sofa, scarcely taking in highlights of Nottingham Forest and some other club that the commentator, Barry Davies, clearly preferred – West Ham or Spurs or some such underachieving Londoners whose devil-may-care approach appealed to Barry's cultured sensibility, prompting adjectives like 'delightful' and 'refreshing'.

Unfortunately for Barry, Forest pinched two second-half beauties without reply. The culprit was a pup with a bowl hairstyle of whom I'd never heard. He was, in truth, precisely the kind of oik I would otherwise have automatically found repugnant. But his pace on the break and two-footed tackles and disrespect for respected opponents and lippy attitude to the gentleman in black were all getting on Barry's wick, and so I warmed to the kid. I thought to myself, momentarily, 'He'll go far.' But the name, when it was eventually said, made no impact because it's rare where I come from. And so that's as far as it went. I may even have been about to drift off. Then this kid scored his second and was running back to his own half for the re-centre when Davies uttered five unforgettable words: '. . . the young man from Cork . . .'

I spent the next two years willing him towards Liverpool. The rags-to-riches edition of his programme biog had him writing to every club in the football league for a trial. If this were true, we agreed, heads had to roll. He was Liverpool momentarily in the eyes of his Forest club captain. Stuart Pearce, in his autobiography *Psycho*, recalls missing that game and later being told by one of the backroom staff that Roy Keane did well on the right wing. Pearce had never heard of him and assumed the name belonged to some new signing at Anfield. Graeme Souness, recognising a midfielder after his own heart, attempted to snare him in 1992 in a straight swap for Dean Saunders. Clough almost choked on his Scotch. Then Clough jumped before anyone could push him, Forest went down and I wrote a letter to Souness, begging him to write the big cheque.

No, really. There comes a time when a man must make one cringing admission. This, if only to illustrate how strongly I felt on the subject, is mine. In my defence, writing letters of advice or admiration to famous people isn't something I did or do. Come to think of it, that was the gist of the letter's opening sentence: 'Dear Mr Souness, I don't usually . . .' He had a clutch of gifted kids hovering in the wings. All they needed was a bit of mettle in the middle. Despite his hard-man billing, I thought Souness seemed approachable. He had starred in Alan Bleasdale's *Boys from the Blackstuff*. He had given Yosser Hughes his autograph and the remains of his champagne. Come to think of it, I may even have addressed him by his first name and followed it with a weedy parenthetic '(if I may)'. I got the number from directory inquiries. The receptionist stifled a laugh. I cashed five pounds into fifties in Spar and called for the address from the payphone in our flat. The woman on the Anfield switch had to repeat herself more than once between the pips and clunking silver. I typed it on the portable my mother bought me, four times because Tippex didn't look classy, and waited.

We spent the summer of 1993 in Oslo. My girlfriend, and soon to become my wife, had a three-month placement in the Norwegian National History Museum. I tagged along on a lark. We had one room in a student block in the woods on the northern edge of the city. Each morning she got the tram downtown and I legged it over to the communal TV room to switch on the Ashes on BBC World before my German nemesis had managed to get ensconced. At drinks on the first morning of the Headingley Test in July, they went back to the studio. 'Sport,' the newscaster announced, 'and Manchester United have this morning unveiled their record signing.' They cut over to footage of microphones and a hundred lenses shutting. I uttered one sharp instinctive 'fuck' and stormed from the communal TV room for ever to the backing track of Fritz guffawing. To this day I await a reply, and an explanation, on Liverpool headed paper.

The pain of that announcement, suffered stoically more or less, has been blunted in the intervening decade by the belief that it was never going to happen any other way. Alex Ferguson saw Roy's worth straight off and tailed him almost three years. United scout Les Kershaw was in the stands in Anfield and reported back. Ferguson went especially to Maine Road a few weeks later to watch him in the flesh. The morning after Forest played at Old Trafford, a mere month into his first pro season, Ferguson phoned the City ground and Clough didn't wait to be told the reason. When Ferguson read in the papers that he had written to every club in the football league for a trial and got only one response, a reign of terror swept through the scouting applications office until it was established that United was the one club to which Roy didn't apply, because he didn't think he was good enough. That alone suggests the higher regard in which he held United. All his family were United and once Ferguson called him at his family home the contest was effectively over.

53

At the end of June 2002 Roy takes his family on holiday in Portugal, and so does Stan. Inevitably, as these things go, they cross each other's paths one sightseeing afternoon in some village square. Roy has been trying to seem chilled about the whole World Cup mayhem. He has more important things to think about, mostly concerning United's new signings and the Champions' League. But in truth he feels cut off from his old life. He feels as if all bridges are burned and there he is, alone on the wrong side. Scratch the surface and he's just as liable to kick off into the same old machine-gun rant about how right he was and how wrong they were.

There is too much old ground to be contested before a basic handshake and 'How are you?' is possible. Each mumbles into his wife's ear who they have just seen on the other side of the square. Each cuts their afternoon short, and bundles the kids into the hired car with bribes of ice cream at the next stop down the line. This is possibly the last chance to make amends.

In the third week of July, United arrive in Dublin for a pre-season friendly with Irish league holders, Shelbourne. Ten thousand fans turn out to drown the boos with choruses of 'There's only one Keano'. At the front of the main stand there are T-shirts on sale that read: 'Michael Collins and Roy Keane – Two Great Cork Leaders Shot in the Back'. Bertie Ahern pays a flying visit. United win 5–0. Halfway through the second half, Roy is substituted. On the touchline he feigns a tantrum, throwing a tracksuit top to the ground. On the way back to the team bus one fan gives him what he later calls 'the dickhead sign'. This is the only memory he will take away from the afternoon.

54

Roy made his Irish debut in a home friendly with Chile at the back end of his first Forest season. May 1991. By then he had become the object of affection that was, even by our affected standards, unusual. Those were the innocent days when players still stepped forward onto the edge of the red carpet, one by one, to wave in sync with their called names. By the time the PA came to him we had all read the story. How he was almost left on the shelf. How, when other nineteen year olds were being advised to consider alternative careers, he was granted one chance and grasped it with an endearing desperation to please. There was the unspoken sense that he was also one of our own more than most, a muddle of stubbornness and vulnerability, shuddering into tackles and blushing when odd shots went askew. He was that *rara avis* who rose from League of Ireland hopelessness to the national side. He even had the neck to tell the FAI where to stick his first call-up and Jack, by all accounts, was overheard referring to him as 'a little bastard'. Suddenly, here he was in green. 'No. 6 Roy Keane' was greeted with a huge cheer. It finished 1–1.

In footage of one of his earliest international goals, Stan is all over him, looking like a man whose kid brother had just scored. Stan's delight is that of someone whose own generation, after years on the periphery, is arriving at the centre. From the terrace, they seemed close. They were drinking buddies. That over-exposed yarn about the last day of the summer tour of the USA, 1992 – they say Roy brought this up in the team meeting. He was with Stan. A few times around that period the Ireland squad trained and stayed in Dundalk in international weeks. There is a photo in Mark Evans's *There's Only One Keano* that must have been taken around then, of Ireland's rising star posing with a renowned coach of underage teams called Jackie Henry. There were lots of stories flying around about wild nights. His youthful mug still adorns the walls of several hostelries in town.

In USA 1994 Stan started all our matches but struggled terribly in the heat. After the 0–0 draw with Norway that saw us into round two, Jack quipped, 'Stan was gone by the end of the national anthem.' Roy was voted Ireland's best player. Despite that, a couple of things suggested that all was not well. Firstly, something a teenager said in a shop in a midlands market town on the day of the FA Cup Final against Chelsea. We travelled there and back by bus to be at the launch of a museum dedicated to the Great Famine. During the speeches I stepped out onto the street to get a score. I asked this lad in a sweet shop.

'Four-nil.'

'Keane score?'

'No, thank God.'

'Sorry?'

The other was a press conference during the World Cup of that summer, given by Gary Kelly, Phil Babb and Jason McAteer. They had been christened the Three Amigos by the Irish press, and were responding to questions about their friendship and their cheeky-chappie popularity. At one point they were asked if Roy, younger than two of them but already a senior member of the squad, was one of the gang. McAteer eventually ended the smirks and embarrassed silence by saying something like, 'Emmm, Roy's a bit different.'

What, we all wanted to know, made Roy 'a bit different'? Shyness, you suspected, and a ferocity born of shyness. He lacked the looks and charm his team-mates had in spades. He also lacked anything resembling a friendship with members of the Irish management. When Jack needed a fall guy to protect his captain, Andy Townsend, after Townsend and Jack's assistant, Maurice Setters, had a bust-up on the training ground in Orlando, he looked no further. Roy stood through the press conference, confused and furious, while Jack informed the cameras there was no rift and Maurice linked his arm around the player's waist and said he'd happily take the lad dancing.

When McCarthy succeeded Charlton as Irish manager in 1996, most of the Liverpool greats had cashed their chips. The only Irish players at Anfield were, ironically, two-thirds of the Three Amigos: McAteer and Babb. Roy Evans, Souness's successor, had signed both of them within eighteen months of USA 1994. He had also signed Mark Kennedy from Millwall, then managed by Mick McCarthy. My guess is, Roy developed his own red/green colour blindness. He started to anticipate Ireland matches with much the same contempt and dread that he anticipated clashes with Liverpool. He knew he was better, and yet guessed his obsessiveness was the butt of a fair percentage of their gags. He played in only one of MacCarthy's first ten internationals in charge, thus prompting the belief that he cared more about playing in red than in green.

55

Mr Roy Keane has gone AWOL. It's official. I am in the kitchen on the first Sunday of August, trying to locate both a tin-opener strong enough to release some *gésiers de canard* and flitting back and forth through the Gs of my Langenscheidt French-English, when Tommy mopes in with a worried puss.

'Dad?'

'Yes?'

'Have you seen Mr Roy Keane?'

'Sure.'

He is thrilled. He has inherited his mother's brains and most of his father's more irritating traits, including a complete helplessness when it comes to finding anything. Time was when he chimed in with his mother's sarcastic refrain at my expense: 'It's gone, it's lost for ever, we'll have to buy a new one', and giggled when whatever was lost was being juggled behind my back. Now, if something has been out of his field of vision for more than ten minutes, and however enormous and impossible to lose that thing might be, he slumps on the couch in the sitting room and tuts at ever-decreasing intervals.

'Where?'

'*Where*? With you.'

'No. Have you seen him in the last few days?'

'I have of course.'

'Where?'

'*Gizzards.*'

'Where?'

'Jesus!'

'Thanks a lot.'

Mr Roy Keane was here or hereabouts all through the World Cup. He went to school for the Germany game, but definitely came back because his backside was attached with a safety pin to the white of the tricolour. After Saudi Arabia he was on the brink of a name change. Asked what I thought of 'Mr Robbie Keane', my absent-minded 'Hmmm' was mistaken for disapproval. Between normal and extra time against Spain I went upstairs for a leak and found him face down in the basin of the en suite shower, like a wino drowning his sorrows. He was his usual smiling self in the candlelit procession on Bastille Day in the old town of Agde. He was ever present on the beach and hung out every evening pegged to the clothes line on the roof terrace. The morning we left, the kids' main job was to ensure their toys got packed. Between us we can't confirm a single positive sighting of him after that point.

We've checked out his usual watering holes: The Toy Trunk, The Linen Basket, The Island Unit Wine Rack, The Liverpool Duvet Cover, The Glove Compartment. We've quizzed those in his immediate menagerie most likely to see him: Teddy, the Alien with alien babies wrapped inside its head, Dingly Zebra and Buzz Lightyear minus one leg. Nothing. Tommy's grandmother, acting as Interpol, has ransacked her spare room in case Mr Roy Keane took advantage of a Sunday afternoon visit to break for the border under an assumed identity. No joy.

Tommy gives up hope. He is convinced Mr Roy Keane got left behind in France. Our landlord said the family arriving immediately after us was Dutch and our son has decided their sons are torturing his rag doll as revenge for Holland not qualifying for Korea/Japan.

'But they won't know his name.'

'They will. He'll tell them.'

'I doubt that very much.'

'Anyway, it says "Ireland" on his jersey.'

'Does it?'

'Yeah.'

'*Oh.*'

I can't help myself. The first chance I get, I draw comparisons between Mr Roy Keane's disappearance and that of his namesake from the public glare. For ten days the real Roy was splattered all over TV and radio news bulletins. By all accounts he even made front page of the *Delhi Times*. His movements were reduced to a handful of sightings during the World Cup. Then nothing for weeks. There are strange emblematic echoes, I suggest, in the fact that Mr Roy Keane has gone underground too, as if the parallel destinies of man and mannequin are merging.

'That's crap,' Tommy says.

'Think about it.'

'No.'

'Pass no remarks to your father,' my wife laughs. 'He's just being *poetic*.'

We pack to drive west for a fortnight. The checklist has been ticked through. The car is teeming with pillows and books. My wife and daughter are waiting. I go to shout upstairs from the front door and hear Tommy's small feathery voice in one of the bedrooms: 'Keano, Keano . . .'

56

'Most soccer fans,' Ian Hamilton wrote, 'need to get hooked on the fortunes of a single player, to build a team around him, so to speak.'

Roy would never play for us. On Tommy's second birthday I bought the smallest Liverpool top on the market, with 'Fowler 9' on the back. He wore it until his belly button was visible and my wife put it away in a drawer with other outgrown garments of sentimental value. Recently, just before we moved house, she called from the top of the stairs, 'What will I do with this?' It seems as if I can place every significant event of the early years of our marriage, day and date and month, through a Fowler goal (although I wouldn't dream of telling her that). When I came out into the hall she had what looked like a red hanky in her hand. It was too small for either of ours and, since the player the Kop had christened 'God' had been flogged to Leeds, of no use to any other kids.

What do you do when your two favourite players play for the arch rivals and, you suspect, have nothing but contempt for each other? My soft spot for bad boys meant that I didn't relish most Liverpool–United encounters in the second half of the nineties. Faced with a choice between satisfied regret (a Liverpool loss in which Roy played a stormer, too many in the mid-nineties) and rueful satisfaction (a Liverpool win in which Fowler scored, a few in recent years), I chose to take the kids to the park around noon two Saturdays a season. In retrospect, I realise I developed a dream combination whereby Keane was excluded through minor injury, there was at least one vintage Fowler strike and Liverpool took all points.

One game stands out. The FA Cup Final of May 1996, usually remembered only for Liverpool's white Armani suits that made them look like Cornettos, for being one of those games that are so poor you stop caring who wins, and for Cantona's peculiar double-jointed winner five minutes from time. I watched it in a tiny pub just south of the border, in the fishing village in which we were living. We were about twenty grown men sardined into four square yards of stoolless floor space. Roy ran the show. A man who looked like Humpty Dumpty in a tennis shirt with a canary yellow sweater tied around his shoulders said so several times for all ears. He and his buddies had that flushed look of men who had come straight from the links to the pub.

'Keane's the boss here,' Humpty Dumpty kept roaring. 'Roy Keane is running this show.'

Everyone wanted to ask him to put a sock in it. But he was right. When Ferguson came onto the pitch after the final whistle and was told by an interviewer who man-of-the-match was, he replied hoarsely, 'I'm not surprised.' On the way back up to the house I remembered blubbing on the steps of my grandfather's greenhouse after they beat us in the 1977 final. The satisfied regret of this time round was better. The house was full of boxes. For years we were convinced we'd be tenants for life; now we had just bought in town and were due to roll the wagons any day. When I stepped in, nicely, my wife said, 'You don't look too cut up.' She'd heard the result on the radio. Tommy had just turned one and Eve was a month. I fed him his tea, something in a bowl that looked like blended mouse.

'We lost,' I told him, 'but Roy played a blinder.'

'Keep making those noises,' my wife said, 'and he'll grow up a United fan.'

'Never! No son of mine . . .'

57

Sometime around the middle of August one of my brothers is in Cork on business, and has to hail a city centre taxi. To fill the silence, he raises the issue of Roy. At this end of the summer the subject has become one of the easiest ways of sizing up someone else. Implicitly, it asks 'What side is your bread buttered?' and mostly there is no certainty what the answer will be. But this is Roy's home patch, Ireland's so-called republican capital. So my brother assumes the driver is on our side, and is less guarded with his phrasing than he might usually be. To his amazement, the driver replies, 'Ah, Roy's a spoilt bollocks.'

'How do you figure that?'

He is laughing inwardly at his luck to stumble upon the only Lee-sider in living memory to be pro-Mick and have no qualms saying so.

'That fuss about the balls . . . Sure, couldn't they have gone down to the nearest supermarket and bought a bagful?'

We are in Galway on 20 August, the evening Ireland hockeys Finland in a pre-season friendly in Helsinki. One of our three goals is scored by Colin Healy, the Corkman originally down to fill Roy's boots in the World Cup squad. We are having dinner in my wife's sister's house. The game is playing on two tellies in separate rooms. I go down to the garden to juggle a ball for almost all of the second half. Twice Tommy appears on the patio, shouting, 'Dad, we scored again. Come in, Dad. You're missing it.'

58

Graeme Souness sold Stan to Aston Villa in 1991, where he held the line alongside Paul McGrath for seven seasons. He was bought back again in 1998 by Roy Evans, in the hope that his experienced head might stop Liverpool leaking sucker punches. When Gerard Houllier succeeded Evans, Stan went back to Villa on a free transfer after a period on loan to Crystal Palace. Houllier had noticed certain players doing impersonations of Evans and parking in the manager's spot. Jason McAteer, it was rumoured, was one of them and Blackburn were prepared to make an offer for him. Kennedy had already been flogged to Wimbledon and Babb was considering a loan to Tranmere Rovers.

Roy waited seven years to exact unholy revenge on Jason's 'Roy's a bit different' sideswipe during that Orlando press conference. The occasion was our away qualifier in Nicosia, March 2001. It was one of those bizarre games we won 4–0 but could easily have lost. Roy scored two, our first and last. His second came in the eighty-seventh and was remarkable for the dismissive manner with which he walked the ball from the corner flag into their box and across the line. 'With a player like that,' blubbed the Cyprus manager Stavros Popadopoulos, 'there is nothing you can do.'

By that stage Roy had three Premiership and two FA Cup medals. He had also graduated from being perennial *enfant terrible* to national hero getting cheered onto chat shows. In retrospect, this was one beatification that was never going to last. All those awards and handshakes and dicky bows weighed heavily on a painfully shy personality. By his own admission, Roy 'dreaded the prospect of international weeks'. He was, according to several reports, battling the bottle. He had made his complaints about the Irish set-up through proper channels and little had changed. Something had to snap.

The Cyprus game was Roy's fiftieth cap. Asked what this milestone meant to him in absolute terms, he replied, 'Absolutely nothing.' Added to that was the bitter fact that we were crap, and McAteer crapper than anyone. The captain took obvious pleasure in his team-mate's complete inability to put a foot right. There were moments when commentator and summariser were prattling only to drown the more colourful running commentary on the pitch. Roy bullied McAteer for seventy-seven painful minutes, way beyond the point where a sympathetic pat on the backside was clearly the better option. When the latter was substituted, the decision seemed one predicated on mercy rather than a tactical switch and the player's lower lip was visibly wobbling. After the game both announced they were considering retirement from international football: McAteer out of sheer lack of self-belief;

Roy, he said, out of frustration with the ineptitude of the FAI. Behind the justification of his many particular gripes, you sensed, was a more general ennui. He wanted out. He, least of all, liked the monster that playing for his country was turning him into.

59

The middle of the fourth week of August. Well and truly holidayed, I am in the pet food aisle in Tesco. Things have simmered down a little. By this stage the meat counter assistant and I have not so much patched things up as reached a point where we can exchange embarrassed smiles of recognition. Still burned in parts that were not made to see the open air, head addled with all that heat, I have mislaid the spirit of the cause if not the cause itself.

I have been wheeling a trolley around with no great purpose other than to avoid an old schoolmaster glimpsed in the distance. A scholar of Latin and mathematics who must have wondered weekly how he found himself undertaking mainly admin duties in a state school in a butt-end provincial town in the early eighties: even to an eleven-year-old he clearly existed adrift of his 'peers'.

He had been a golfer, albeit a golfer from an era when golf was a civilised stroll through barely cultivated dunes, towing a pencil-slim bag after a ball the size of a marble. And because his own son showed promise, and because there were a few other families of a similar persuasion, he set up a school team. I think his folly was let go only to indulge an austere senior staff member on the home straight.

His team became Irish champions. His son, one of my brothers who later turned pro, and a third who was pretty talented were the best school team in the country by a country mile. To my knowledge, their win remains the only national title the school can claim in any sport. To those of us who came in its immediate wake, it was enough to justify a hatful of school days off in a minibus, free golf and a basket of chicken and chips in the clubhouse. There would be a further provincial title and a smattering of other minor cups to which even I contributed. In the intervening twenty years or so, those four or so years in sunlight got replayed in his head as some prelapsarian golden age.

Mostly, I am glad to pass the time of day with the last man on the planet who looks at me and sees a fair-to-middling golfer. But it is always the same story, and it can lop an hour or two off your speckled span. Then I take my eye off the ball and sidle towards the checkout via the pet food aisle. The thought, 'Sir keeps cats' has just occurred when I hear:

'Mr O'Callaghan.'

'Sir.'

There are other teachers I have long since called by the abbreviated versions of their Christian names. There are even a few sad cases I manage to lord it over, twiddling my car keys and exuding an air of either the recently returned or the soon to jet out. But this is different. Despite being thirty-three and the father of two, in his company I revert immediately to that overweight fourteen-year-old, the sullen scrapper who more often than not could be relied upon to bring home an early point from far out on the course. This one requires the full deferential form of address.

'Sir.'

'Mr O'Callaghan.'

We chew the fat, and out of misguided sympathy I steer the conversation at the earliest possible juncture into the glory days of 1982. Usually, this is his favourite historical period and he is only too happy to recount at length the minutiae of balls lost or holes halved. But on this occasion he doesn't bite. In fact, he eyes me with mild derision. He all but says, 'Get over it son, start living in the present.' He has other, bigger fish to fry.

'And as for our friend from Cork . . .'

He has genuinely lost me.

'Who?'

'The World Cup, Mr O'Callaghan.'

I no longer have the stomach for this.

'Reckless,' he says, 'pure reckless.'

I have to coax myself, inwardly, to remember his seniority. I couldn't possibly stand here hectoring him on the story's rights and wrongs. So I take a deep breath and brace myself for an onslaught.

'But he was always reckless. In fact, Mr O'Callaghan, you could argue that it was his very recklessness that made him the player he is, that made him captain of his country. Whereas McCarthy . . .'

This is an unexpected turn in the conversation. I am authentically speechless, although admittedly my speechlessness is academic. This is the first chinwag of the summer in which I haven't been able to get a word in edgeways. My role is to nod along, jaw fractionally agape.

'. . . McCarthy is so stupid he doesn't realise who his best asset is. He forgets just like that . . .' (snaps his fingers) '. . . who he owes most to. Of course our friend from Cork has a short fuse, but that shouldn't have come as news to anybody. McCarthy is such a dumbo he backed him into a corner in front of the rest of his colleagues and never once thought what the consequences would be.'

I had expected the voice of righteous indignation on behalf of authority for authority's sake. For a few moments I stand there glowing, filled with unexpected admiration for my old taskmaster.

'Do you think the manager of this supermarket, if he has a row with one of his staff, will settle it by giving that employee a dressing-down in front of the rest of the staff after closing hours?'

I attempt to answer.

'No, Mr O'Callaghan. No sir. He will do what any good manager should, speak to that staff member privately and get his point across quietly but firmly. And if that staff member happens to be his very best, his prize bull, well . . .'

The right index finger is pointing heavenward, occasionally wagging for emphasis at the end of each point. This could be a lesson in calculus, or the conjugation of irregular Latin verbs. I agree with everything the message is telling me, and yet am getting vaguely seasick amid the rhetoric of its delivery.

'Do you think I ever took a difficult teacher to task in the staff common room, in front of his or her colleagues?'

He laughs maniacally.

'Good Lord, no.'

And on it goes.

There is a great scene in *Taxi Driver*, in which De Niro has to sit through a backseat tirade by one of his customers, played in cameo by Scorsese. The guy is a middle-aged businessman whose wife is playing away. They are parked beneath an apartment, and are getting snatches of action at one of the windows. Scorsese launches into this crazed riff about there being so much sick shit out on the street and how it should all be blown away. De Niro is eyeing him in the rear-view, clearly thinking, 'This guy is nuts.' We have already heard the same tirade from De Niro more than once. Now he hears his own words from someone else's mouth, and doesn't like what he's hearing.

60

The night Fowler's transfer was announced, a fortnight after we qualified for the World Cup, me and Tommy had our first football quarrel worthy of the description. I kept asking the screen, 'How can they justify selling him?'

'They have Michael Owen.'

Tommy loves Michael Owen. I liked him well enough when he was understudy to God, even if he always came with the prefect-in-waiting's clean-shaven whiff. Then Houllier made it clear his first-choice striker would be Owen, who in turn dropped heavy hints his preferred partner was a lethargic sprinter called Emile Heskey.

'But that's not the same.'

'It's better.'

'I beg your pardon.'

'Owen's better.'

'Owen's better than Fowler?'

'Fowler's crap.'

'Excuse me.'

'He's not crap. He's just too old.'

Tommy didn't realise my voice was lifting.

'And all the goals he scored?'

'What goals?'

'*What goals* . . .'

'I don't remember many.'

'He's scored over a hundred and seventy goals for Liverpool.'

'Not many lately.'

'That's because he can't get a game.'

'That's because Owen's better.'

'You disloyal little frigger.'

These days Tommy loves Robbie Keane. I like Robbie well enough, but will never get around the idea of him as Roy's tribute act. Every time the Irish fans sing 'Keano-o, Keano-o . . .' I think of Charlie Chaplin, in old age, entering a Charlie Chaplin Lookalike Contest. He lost. During the Saudi match Ron Atkinson, summarising on ITV, said how he thought Roy Keane should stay out on the right. He meant Robbie, but for a second I felt like a man waking to the relief that it had all just been a sickening dream. That evening Tommy scored goal after exultant goal between two staked saplings on the green area in front of our house. After each, he ran away to the pebble-dashed wall copying the bow-and-arrow celebration Robbie did after his goal. I was holding on the phone, and watched him through the open door. His actions were not so much those of an archer, but rather an old boy playing the button accordion at a wedding.

Perhaps football is one of the last privileges of youth, something you cling on to longer than decency advises. Your idolatry renews itself for a few decades. Then you wake up and realise your team is populated with pups who can't play and you don't like. Your favourites have aged as much as you have, or been sold to scrapyard clubs like Middlesborough and Aston Villa. The day that happens, football is lost to you. Our old man used to be nuts about Leeds. He loved Johnny Giles. By the time we were equally nuts about Liverpool he couldn't have named two players in the Leeds first eleven. After Fowler's transfer, I wasted the rest of the 2001/2 season wishing Liverpool to lose and the Kop to turn against the manager. After Roy was sent home from the World Cup, I watched Ireland's games with little interest. When they were eliminated, the only emotion I felt was relief. Theoretically, the point of supporting football teams is that you want them to win. Can you still claim to be a fan when you want them to lose? I call this the Johnny Giles Syndrome.

61

In the third week of August, extracts of Roy's autobiography are serialised in the *News of the World* and *The Times*. Much is made of his account of his infamous tackle on Alf Inge Haaland in the Manchester derby in April 2001, in which he admits to premeditation. A statement from the FA says that the association will wait 'to see the book in its full context before making any decisions'. Roy says he isn't losing any sleep over the matter. At a press conference in Hungary before United's Champions' League qualifier, Alex

Ferguson admits that United's solicitors 'perused' the proofs before it went to print. He says, 'I don't think Roy has anything to worry about. I don't think there's a case to answer.'

Eamon Dunphy publicly ends thirty years of friendship with Johnny Giles. Giles has been critical of Keane on the brewing Haaland issue. Dunphy brands Giles a 'hypocrite' in the *Mirror* and alleges that he knowingly broke another professional's leg while playing for Leeds in 1965. Giles denies the allegations. They continue to appear in tandem on the Irish version of *The Premiership*, albeit with banter at a premium.

At teatime on the last day of the month, Saturday the 31st, the third week of the new Premiership season, my younger brother calls. He asks without saying hello, 'Did you hear the news?'

'What news?'

'Roy was sent off at Sunderland.'

'Serious?'

'Sounds as if himself and McAteer had a scrap.'

It's all over the main evening news, both on RTÉ and BBC. The pair had clashed earlier in the second half, and McAteer was seen to make obvious book taunts. In injury time, Roy clipped him with his elbow, was manhandled by ref Uriah Rennie, and Jason lay on the deck clutching his ear like a sunbather singing harmonies. On his way to the bench Roy passed Niall Quinn coming on as a sub. Niall shook his hand and tried to say something, only to be blasted by a mouthful of asterisks from Sir Alex. It finished 1–1. In the *Observer* next morning he is 'Mad for It', for the *Mail on Sunday* this is just another instalment in 'Keane's Red Rage Shame' and he is still the *News of the World*'s favourite 'Nutter!' Thus the Keane season reopens.

PART III

Penalties

Hey Roy! It's brother against brother, father against son, hack against hack in this never-ending war you started.

Tom Humphries,
Laptop Dancing and the Nanny Goat Mambo

62

Roy's book, Niall's, and Mick's World Cup diary amount to a series of narratives as daft as they are unreliable, what Keith Duggan calls in the *Irish Times*: 'Irish soccer producing an entire generation of literary figures in one month'.

Roy Keane: The Autobiography has scarcely a kind word to say about Roy Keane. His is not benign, bashful self-deprecation. It is the shy man's rage at himself. At times you sense he is being more blunt than honest. There is lots about drink, for example, but almost nothing that addresses his decision to pack it in. His view of the game, and his place in it, is dispiritingly prosaic. Variations of the phrase 'getting the job done' appear with frightening frequency. His ghost Eamon Dunphy has always had an insider's desperation to have you believe everything – professional football, tiddlywinks, wok cuisine – is 'savage, cruel, relentlessly punishing'. In fact, there are whole paragraphs in which the ghost's voice seems to be audible. It's like being hectored through frosted glass. You hope it's a meeting of minds, if only to suppress the suspicion that our great warrior has become the ventriloquist's wooden dummy mouthing someone else's wooden lines.

Did the process of putting together the book act as a catalyst in what finally came to pass in the last week of last May? Roy has told BBC Sport that he was working on the book from September 2001. Niall says that when Roy stood to speak in the Hyatt ballroom he spoke calmly as if his and Mick's mutual history – Boston 1992 and 'every incident and perceived slight since then' – were an A–Z. It is entirely possible that having to recollect those events over the winter prior to Korea/Japan unnecessarily aggravated old minor grievances that had otherwise lain dormant for most of a decade.

Piecing together that catalogue, its instances of isolation, may well have helped to bring him to the end of his international tether.

The most remarkable thing about *Niall Quinn: The Autobiography* is the extent to which it is about Roy Keane. To judge from the ratio between those pages given over to the days of late May 2002, and those on the rest of his life, one could be forgiven for calculating that about twenty-three of Niall's thirty-five years in this mortal coil have been whiled away on the island of Saipan. In its pages Niall constantly defines himself in comparison with, and in opposition to, his former colleague. The Roy he sees 'rails against failure and rages for success . . . despise[s] the rest of us for not having the same brooding, obsessive passion'. And he reckons that Roy in turn sees him 'as too soft, too nice, too much of a goody goody, too damn happy . . . football's version of the Singing Nun'. When Niall and Staunton went to Keane's room immediately after the bust-up, they were flustered and emotional and he was 'like steel'.

The subtext is happiness. Much as Niall would have us believe that he too has seen the dark side, it does not wash. The come-all-ye fireside ramble ('Let me tell you something about my dad, a Tipperary hurler'; 'Let me tell you about my friend . . . a young lad from Dublin . . . he's HIV positive') is entirely consistent with the fact that the Quinns' siring stallion is called 'Cois na Tine' (literally, 'beside the fire'). Where Roy confines himself to one charmless aphorism – 'Happiness is not being afraid' – the word litters the pages of Niall's book like spent cartridges:

> I don't have millions and I don't have many medals but I'm happy . . . Almost twenty years in the game and I'm still as happy as when I started. That's the secret – being happy.

If there is as much about Roy in Niall's book as there is about Niall, then there is as much about golf in Mick McCarthy's *Ireland's World Cup 2002* as there is about football. In December 2001 Mick travelled to Busan for the World Cup draw, and then on to investigate Saipan. He was accompanied by Ray Treacy, travel agent to the FAI, and Eddie Corcoran, the liaison officer. What finally clinched the decision was the 76 Mick shot on the championship course designed by former US Open winner Larry Nelson, and the local burghers' promises to prepare a football pitch to fairway standard:

> Considering I shoot a very low round on Coral Ocean Point and take the money off Ray Treacy, I will be more than happy if the pitch is up to that standard.

It was with great regret that Mick couldn't participate in the 'Texas Scramble' organised on the same course by Ian Evans for the rest day. His back was playing up and he had to content himself with an hour on the bike. At the same time, his captain was signing his death warrant in the company of two of Ireland's leading sports writers. By the squad meeting convened for 7.30pm the following evening, Mick had received an Internet printout of the *Irish Times* interview. And the source of the printout? '*Irish Independent* journalist, Philip Quinn,' Mick writes, 'someone I regularly take money off on the golf course.'

63

Scarcely a day passes since the World Cup that Tommy hasn't drawn a football picture for me. The whole month of July in France, and every day before dinner I was presented with a line drawing of an Ireland game that had the dedication 'To Dad love Tommy'. One afternoon, during an August fortnight in Spiddal, I heard him ranting at his cousin Deidre in the back seat of the car. It was, of course, his father's speech, word for sickening word. This has gone too far, I thought to myself.

In September, in the first Euro 2004 qualifying match, we lose away to Russia. I am secretly delighted, but give a pretty convincing display of head-holding. The scenario – a fiasco in Eastern Europe, a comeback scuppered by a late o.g. – reminds me of being a kid.

I begin to wonder about the value of what I have passed on to Tommy. His pre-match butterflies are starting earlier with each game. He sits there, on his hands, on the big armchair, with his tricolour dangling on its bamboo stake. His flushed expression goes through various levels of agony. He looks the way my brothers and I must have looked at his age. The only difference is that we were schooled on defeat, and knew instinctively how to deal with it. His, I suppose, is the first generation of Irish fans weaned on success. He sings 'You'll never beat the Irish' down to the final whistle. Then he looks at me, confused, as if it is my fault.

The drawings keep coming. The most recent depicts a version of Robbie Keane's goal against Iran in the first leg of the play-off at Landsdowne Road. There are only a handful of players on the pitch, all of them Irish except for a levitating Iranian keeper, all of them face on. The trajectory of the ball, from Shay Given's boot to Robbie Keane's head and into the net, is marked in wobbly widening tramlines. For some reason, Gary Breen is right beside Robbie, smiling, arms above his head. Roy takes centre stage. He is twice as tall as any of the others. He has a mop of curly hair, and he too is smiling ear to ear.

64

Benny says that Eamon Dunphy's cut for ghosting Roy's auto-biography was two million sterling. The man himself received three. I know for a fact that Benny's estimates have overshot the mark by at least one nought. But even I think my more reliable information is less compelling than my barber's extravagant hearsay.

'Two fuckin' million, that's what Dunphy got. Two million and a house in France.'

'A house in France?'

At the end of the World Cup one of the tabloids ran an exposé on Dunphy's newly acquired villa in Deauville, Normandy. While the article did claim that the maison had been bought with his cut of the advance, there was never any suggestion that it had been given to him as a sweetener.

'Keane gave him his house in France. "I don't want it," he said, "away you go my son." '

I ask him if he has bought the book. He sniffs.

'Is that a no?'

Two of his colleagues down the line start coughing theatrically.

'Benny, you didn't?'

'We have to know the facts,' he blushes. 'And the fact is, Keane's a tramp.'

'A tramp you don't mind giving your hard-earned to.'

The thought that he is lining the devil's pockets has clearly never dawned on Benny. For several moments he seems on the brink of uttering a piece of classic repartee that dissipates in sighs. I put him out of his misery, broaching the national team. What did Benny make of the Moscow mauling?

'A bad day at the office, that's all.'

'That's exactly what Mick said.'

'What?'

'At the post-match press conference Mick said it had been a bad day at the office.'

'He was right. God help the Swiss next month.'

Everybody has bought the book. It has already become the biggest selling hardback in Irish publishing history. The carpenter's apprentice who fits the boards upstairs in our new house has bought it. It's one of two books he owns. The other is *The Silence of the Lambs*. Small World looks as if he queued outside the shop. I drive past a few mornings and he has it in one hand, lollipop stick in the other, and is addressing a gathering of mums like some latter-day evangelist on the godless front line. I avoid him as long as I can. I think I know already what he is going to say and can only guess at the length of its saying. Then one nippy morning he collars me on foot and demands, 'Have you got it yet?'

Tommy got it for me for my thirty-fourth birthday. He saw it in the window of the shop in which he gets his stickers and his monthly Liverpool comic, and begged my wife. For a week they dropped hints not heavy enough for my thick skull and winked across rooms. She thought I knew and was just playing along. I didn't. Then the evening before the happy day she came home and found me keying in an email to the editor of a magazine, offering to review it with the sole purpose of wangling a free copy. 'Jesus,' she said, 'you're slow.' Its beautifully gift-wrapped oblong was on the breakfast table next morning.

'One word,' Small World says. 'Cantona.'

'*Cantona.*'

'He adored Cantona, everything the man did.'

'Good for him.'

'You're missing the point, Liverpool.'

'Enlighten me.'

'What happened to Cantona's international career?'

In the coming weeks, I will repeat this many times as my own insight.

'Oh yeah,' I say. 'You're right.'

'Small world.'

'Small world indeed.'

I go back to it that night. I even underline. Roy's reverence of Cantona is amazing. Again, it is shy Paddy selling his own skills short and mooning admiringly at a champagne-quaffing Pierre who had the ball on a string. He admires especially Cantona's capacity to present an enigmatic exterior to the media and yet be one of the lads. Their careers at Old Trafford are inextricable. Ferguson bought them within eight months of each other. One was sent off in the FA Cup semi-final against Crystal Palace in 1995 and attacked a fan on the way, and the other saw red against the same team two weeks later for stamping Gareth Southgate. Both were fined and suspended. In the final moments of the FA Cup Final in 1996, the man-of-the-match tore strips off the goal scorer for showboating. The captain's armband passed between them, and the mantle of existentialist bootboy. To the author of *Keane: The Autobiography*, his predecessor remains the embodiment of class.

When Saipan happened we all looked to more obvious precedents: Stefan Effenberg sent home from USA 1994 for giving the German fans a close-up of his middle finger; Edgar Davids getting his marching orders in England 1996 after racial bloodletting in the Dutch camp ended with the player telling a radio interviewer that the manager should take his head out from the backsides of his white colleagues. Nobody, however, pointed to Cantona. Then in the first week of June the *Star* reported that Eric, in England for a beach-football tournament, voiced his support of his old team-mate. 'I think Roy Keane is too professional for Ireland,' he said, 'because they are amateurs . . . who do not understand these kind of players.' It should have dawned then. Cantona had been banned from his national team for (forgive my French) fucking its manager off from an unmerciful height.

The occasion was a match between Marseilles and Strasbourg in 1989. Cantona had been having a hard time both with club and country. That night, however, he played like a god. He came to the post-match interview hair wet, unshaven, in denim jacket, and got carried away. Asked about his relationship with the French manager, he said:

I was reading an article by Mickey Rourke, who is a guy I really like, and he referred to the people who awarded the Oscars in Hollywood as shit bags. Well, I think Henry Michel is not far from being in that category.

Cantona was banned and was subjected to several newspaper analyses by France's leading psychologists. He remained in the wilderness until Michel was sacked after a draw in Cyprus scuppered qualification to Italia 1990. It was 1–1. Stop me if any of this starts sounding familiar.

65

In his early days at Nottingham Forest, Roy's favourite grub was kebabs. On the evidence of his book, he learned to associate junk food with the hassle he experienced in Cork as Forest's rising star:

> I might be queuing for fish and chips or a kebab (my favourite) when I'd hear someone asking 'Who does he think he is?'

He fails only to express a preference between shish and doner, but does inform us that he returned to Nottingham for his second season a full stone heavier. When he joined United in 1993 he told one reporter, 'I was always a great cheeseburger man but the dietician says it's a minus to eat too many of them.'

Then there is the infamous opening of a new branch of Harry Ramsden's on the Naas Road, long gone down in the annals of Irish football. June 1995, the hottest summer in living memory and the last straw in Big Jack's tenure as boss. The team had two qualifiers for England 1996 in an eight-day period. The first was away to Liechtenstein. It was 0–0. The mortification of that result was captured at the time by the words of Peter Ball in the *Sunday*

Tribune: 'Ireland drew with a mountaintop yesterday.' From there the squad flew to an interim base in Limerick because of an honorary doctorate the city's university was conferring on Jack. The lads were on the tear all week, and got the bus to Dublin for pre-match training on the Friday afternoon.

On the outskirts of the city Jack ordered the driver to take an unscheduled detour. He was one of the shareholders in Harry Ramsden's chain of chippers and had organised some press to come along and snap the national squad launching a new branch. One of the senior players cut a ribbon and then they all sat down in their green tracksuits to fish and chips. Roy was injured again, but he had it on the good authority of both Paul McGrath and Denis Irwin, and says the story kept the dressing rooms of the Premiership in stitches for months after. Gary Kelly achieved cult status by accepting and passing Harry's Challenge: a giant fish and chips with a portion of mushy peas. 'He thought there'd be a certificate,' Niall says, 'but he got a free dessert instead, which he duly ate.' The complimentary sweet suggests that the team had to pay for the rest. Despite Jack's reputation for being 'guarded' with his wallet, that would be hard to believe. Roy claims the precise species was haddock, quite a feat of memory for someone who wasn't there.

We lost against Austria the following afternoon. The Irish players looked as if they were running in quicksand. We had led the group up until then. Another loss away to Austria, a drubbing in torrential rain in Lisbon and a play-off against the Dutch at Anfield spelt curtains. Tony Polster, the scorer of a pair of goals, is a name that still makes older members of the green army wince. That the demise of Jack, angling addict, was precipitated by fried fish is an idea too seasoned with irony for Roy to pass up:

> Yes, Austria won 3–1. Some of the lads reported their legs 'went' twenty minutes from the end. Fucked. But they'd passed Harry's Challenge.

In the summer of 2000 Roy had Mick to his house. This he clearly viewed as a gesture of friendship. 'Nobody gets into my house,' he tells Sean O'Hagan of the *Observer*. He wanted 'a reformed approach': streamlined travel arrangements, first-class seats for players, proper hotels and improved diet in the run-up to big matches. Roy says Mick said, 'Of course, you're right.' Apart from the bones of the story there is little available texture. Did they eat? Did Mick meet his wife and kids, get a tour of the hallowed halls? We do know that Roy told Mick how it was scientifically accepted that pasta, fruit and cereals eaten three hours before a game was the ideal last supper. There is something comical about the idea of the two of them, uneasy in each other's company, discussing linguini, apples and Alpen.

By the opening qualifier for Korea/Japan away to Holland in Amsterdam, Roy thought he had the whole issue of team grub sorted. There was to be a meal in their hotel the night before the game, followed by pre-match in the Ajax stadium. When he arrived in the dining room he found the boys eating cheese sandwiches and approached the top table to see what was happening. Ian Evans, Mick's Welsh right-hand man affectionately known as Taff, said that if anyone had specific food requests all they had to do was ask. Roy thought he had. He stormed back to his (single) room in high dudgeon, phoned down to reception and got a pizza delivered. That evening Mick pulled him to one side in training to ask what was eating him. What was eating him was what he was eating: 'Do you think Jimmy Floyd Hasselbaink is eating fucking cheese sandwiches or takeaway fucking pizza tonight?'

On the Friday in Saipan, when Roy was under siege in his room after the rest of the squad had lifted off to Tokyo, the hotel manager insisted on booking him a taxi and slipping him out the back. In the couple of hours between that call and the taxi arriving, a credit card machine was sent up so Roy could pay off his vast phone bill. There was also a basket of chicken and chips, compliments of the kitchen.

That last detail is gleaned from an interview given to the *Irish Times* on 31 August 2002. In the course of the interview Roy says that 'the Diet Coke and the popcorn and the Minstrels' he got at the pictures 'was the highlight of [his] international weeks under Mick'. Much of the piece dwells on the chalk-and-cheese nature of their relationship. At one point Tom Humphries asks straight out, what in one sentence was it about Mick he couldn't stomach? Roy says:

> I saw him one night on *They Think It's All Over* with Gary Lineker and I'm not trying to run anybody's life, but he's on about eating hairy burgers and all this, and I'm shaking my head, 'Mick, Mick, Mick. You're the Irish manager.'

66

In October my wife travels to a literary festival in Kuala Lumpur. On the last day of the festival the participants are taken by bus to a fishing village to experience a slice of Malaysian life. As luck would have it, just as the readings commence in the square, the first twitchings of the monsoon season begin. Before they know it, there is an almighty downpour. Plan B is thus put into action: a chance to visit an authentic Malaysian house. One by one the participants are buzzed away on the backs of mopeds. My wife, who once saw her sister break her leg on one in Kos, doesn't fancy it. She is last standing under the awning when a car pulls up.

The house she is taken to is just like any bungalow you'd pass in the west of Ireland. The man's name is Poul and he lives with his mother. My wife is offered mango juice and fruit just picked from their garden. Poul runs a restaurant in Kuala Lumpur and has scraps of English. He asks where my wife is from, and what kind of food we eat in Ireland. Pork is the first thing that enters her head.

'Pork,' my wife says.

Poul and his mother squint at her, bewildered.

'*Pok?*'

She mimics a pig's grunt. There is a horrified silence that gets broken a moment later by the stifled giggles of Poul's mum. Then there is silence again. My wife is tired. She wants to repay their hospitality with conversation, but she can think of nothing other than getting home to her family. Poul and his mum sit there staring straight at her, and my wife stares at the paisley patterned carpet on the floor, just like the paisley patterned carpet you'd find on the floor in the living room of any bungalow in the west of Ireland. After what seems like an age, Poul is hit by a bolt of lightning.

'Ireland!' he gasps.

'Yes,' my wife says wearily. 'Ireland.'

'Ireland . . .' Poul is suddenly on the edge of his seat. 'Roy Keane! Ireland! Roy Keane! Roy Keane, and his brother Robbie!'

All summer she has listened with fraying patience to me and Tommy. Suddenly Roy and football throw her a life-ring she happily grabs. They make it last half an hour. Poul and his staff are in a restaurant league. His team is Liverpool. But he loves Roy most. He wishes Roy played for Liverpool. He seems especially aggrieved about the World Cup. He clenches his fists, gently, and starts tapping his temples. Ominously, Poul's mum starts stroking his forearm and whispering words of consolation in Malay.

'McCarteee,' he is whining, 'very bad. Very bad McCarteee . . .'

There is a second when my wife thinks this is a practical joke rigged up by me. The coincidence is too weird. She throws the pair an arched old-fashioned look that tells them the game is up. She forces a chuckle. They seem stunned, and Poul puts his fists down. It was not a practical joke, clearly, but her reaction has defused the situation. After another smaller silence they revert to the original gag about the pig. They say 'Pok, pok', laugh and make grunting noises. Poul drives my wife back to the waiting bus.

We are in stitches about it in Arrivals. Myself and the kids have gone to fetch her early the following morning. She wags her finger the way Poul did, and mimics him shouting, 'Very bad McCarteee.'

<h1 style="text-align:center">67</h1>

Then there's the 'English cunt' business. Somebody has decided that this is one of the phrases Roy threw at Mick. It wasn't, but it's a sensitive area to start digging into. Players raised as Irish people in England were in the room that night and they know it wasn't said.

Niall Quinn, *Niall Quinn: The Autobiogrpahy*

So what was said in the team meeting in the restaurant in Saipan? What was the sequence of events? The accounts of the hero and anti-hero (depending on your allegiance), and those of the silent attendant lords, have already taken their place alongside Essex and Tyrone on the riverbank at Athclynth.

If you take Roy at his word, Mick did most of the running. Roy interrupted to ask if they could continue the conversation in private. Mick had the Humphries interview in his hand and was 'on a roll'. If you take Roy at his word, his speech was brief and came at the very end of proceedings. Niall reckons he went on for about ten minutes, performing 'a feat of oratory, intelligence and some wit' that left the rest of the squad practically lying on the floor, speechless. The *Irish Times* interview was raised only as a last resort, thirty seconds before Roy left the room. Mick has himself giving a public reading from the interview, to illustrate Roy's contempt for his team-mates, and generally giving as good as he got until Roy's *eight*-minute 'rant'.

Did Roy, before storming off, tell Mick to stick the World Cup up his arse? That is the only point on which the pair agree. Paul Howard suggests in *The Gaffers* that Roy actually said, 'Stick it up your bollocks.' Niall seems to have heard none of this. Did Gary Kelly really ask 'Is that it then? Is it really over?' (Quinn)? Did he initiate a round of applause for McCarthy (Howard)? Who was that anonymous squad member who supposedly shouted, 'Mick McCarthy well done' (McCarthy)? Dean Kiely's joke about filling Roy's boots fell flat or was met with nervous laughter or cracked the lads up, depending on whom you believe.

Their versions pale beside those of Matt Holland and Jason McAteer, published in their respective World Cup diaries at the time. Holland, against his better judgement I suspect, corroborated Keane's claim that he requested the discussion be continued behind closed doors and underlined the unreality of events: 'I sat there much like the rest,' he wrote, 'feeling as if the whole thing had been a dream, a surreal dream.' McAteer gave an insight into the cocktail of gratitude and resentment stirred up by playing alongside Roy:

> He said some strange and very hurtful things at the meeting for our benefit . . . And I thought: 'We haven't really made it to the World Cup. We haven't really the right to be here. We owe it all to Roy. And Roy thinks we're shit.'

Only Niall avers to the 'English cunt' myth. Roy has always denied it. He told the *Mail on Sunday* at the end of that week: 'I didn't refer to him being an Englishman, nor an Irishman, in any way.' As recently as September, speaking to Sean O'Hagan in the *Observer*, he still sounded aggrieved that the rumour has been allowed to take hold so easily in football lore:

> It irritated me because people over there could have killed that stuff but they chose not to . . . I have to live in England, and to

be accused of saying that sort of thing it's not nice for my wife and family.

It is, admittedly, rich of Roy to expect a dig-out from the very people who had been at the receiving end of his abuse. That Niall obliges him, despite being personally slighted several times before and since, is credit to his generosity. It also begs the question: where did the rumour originate? It suggests an image of Keane that pre-dated Korea/Japan, coloured by sightings of him in the stand at Celtic matches and by his publicly expressed wish to end his career at Park Head. As far back as 1993, in the midst of his transfer wranglings, he was christened 'Rebel Roy' by certain English newspapers. In that image Keane is disloyal, insular, irregular, beyond the pale. It is also an image that permits writers such as Christopher Davies, in the *Daily Telegraph*, to suggest bizarrely that McCarthy is now 'a victim of mob rule' and 'the fact that he was born in England is probably a factor in [his critics'] vitriol.'

68

Jack had only one tactical idea. Fortunately, it was a good one. It changed international football. In footage of matches from the seventies, defenders in possession stroll out at with all the unhurried freedom of nudists on a beach. Jack was the first to recognise that and, famously, instructed the Irish team to 'put them under pressure'. We loved that. Jack's Geordie accent uttering those words was even sampled into a hit single by U2's drummer, Larry Mullen. Jack was an advocate of the game's eternal intangibles: pressure, pride, passion. All of which are good things, except that they overlook one factor central to soccer: the ball.

According to the Book of Jack, tanned handsome men from

hotter climes were naturally more skilful than us with the ball, but found wanting when it came to argy bargy. Our whole game plan, therefore, was structured around not having the ball. There were matches against big countries when we actually seemed to give it away on purpose, and pinned them back into their own half. It worked. Unfortunately, Jack hadn't a second idea about what to do *with the ball* and so we struggled against minnows. In his reign, we beat England, Spain, Germany, Holland, Italy, but suffered impotent scoreless draws with the likes of Norway, Egypt and Liechtenstein.

Mick encouraged the newer generation to keep possession, to pass. Then they landed in paradise on Saturday, 18 May 2002, to find craters on the pitch, no kits, no salt drinks and no balls. The DHL-couriered skips were still en route. FIFA had released the new Fevernova ball in time for pre-tournament practice and there was word from other camps that it was inclined to play tricks. It finally arrived in the small hours between Sunday and Monday. When Roy complained in interviews later that week, he was perceived to be whingeing needlessly. It was no big deal. Arriving at football's World Cup without footballs was, it seems to me, the logical conclusion of Jack's tactical philosophy.

I am reminded of this rereading the paragraph in *Keane: The Autobiography* that describes his tackle on Alfie Haaland, that has been pounded in the press and that is the basis for the FA's two misconduct charges. It is the only passage of the book I actively dislike, although not for any of the received reasons. It was a very bad tackle, but no worse for being replayed umpteen times on Sky Sports News. I don't mind the language, and I actually admire the admission of intent. It goes against the grain of hypocrisy within the game whereby footballers carry out horrific, premeditated fouls and claim in the tunnel that they slipped. The only bit I find truly depressing is the passing disregard for the ball: it was there or thereabouts he *thinks*.

When did Roy stop noticing the ball? He has always been a ballplayer who does simple things, beautifully. If you think about it, that joke on the team coach in Boston about McCarthy's first touch wouldn't have worked without an unspoken mutual acknowledgement that the joker's was superior. Some of his Irish teammates have been heard to grumble about the pace of his passes, to wonder if he was lording it over them. He has allowed, however, the hard-man image to obscure his skill. He was joint top scorer in the qualifying campaign, for example, and yet you never see clips of his goals. Whenever his name crops up in the news, it gets accompanied by footage of him mowing into some poor unfortunate's heels, as if the ball and its presence were a matter of complete indifference.

Big Jack, more vocal than most in McCarthy's corner during the World Cup, has been conspicuous by his reticence in the past few weeks. Perhaps Jack realises the most obvious precedent involves himself. After the 1970 World Cup, Tyne Tees Television screened a documentary about the Charlton brothers in which the elder admitted to keeping an imaginative 'little black book' of the names of those who had one coming. 'If I get the chance to do them I will,' Jack said. 'I will make them suffer before I pack it in.' Leo McKinstry, author of *Jack & Bobby*, says there was 'a national outcry'. Jack was made to apologise, but the FA saw fit to issue neither fine nor suspension. 'Everyone knows what goes on,' Jack said, 'but no one has ever said it before.'

The FA, having had the chance to bone up, formally charges Roy on two counts of misconduct: for premeditating a dangerous tackle and for publishing an account of the incident for financial gain. Whatever about imitation, this is a case of art superceding life. Not long ago the howls of outrage were about 'the Haaland tackle'. Now it is 'the Haaland paragraph' that gets replayed over and over. On 15 October Roy is accompanied by Eamon Dunphy and Alex

Ferguson to the Reebok Stadium in Bolton. 'I should take the rap, but he won't let me,' Dunphy had told the *Observer*. Roy is cross-examined by John Sturman QC, the three-man panel deliberates for six hours and returns with a fine of £150,000 and a five-match ban to begin on 7 November. The former is the heftiest in league history and the latter makes Roy the only player suspended twice for one tackle.

69

The evening of 16 October, a Wednesday. Me and two of my brothers go out to watch the latest episode in Irish football. For the first time in heaven knows how long a competitive home game is not being broadcast live on national television. The Sky factor has kicked in proper. There are lots of good-humoured double standards being voiced before the whistle. On one level, that we can no longer watch our national team gratis in the comfort of our own homes is (in Arthur Daly's phrase) 'a diabolical liberty of the working man'. On another level, the working man is silently counting his lucky stars to have such a cast-iron excuse to perch on a bar stool midweek.

There is extra pressure on tonight's game, the kind of pressure that doesn't really tally with one away defeat. Mick has been digging his own grave. Firstly, there was the book and its admission that he was 'ecstatic' when Roy decided not to apologise. Like Roy's admission of intent on the Haaland tackle, was that such a surprise? Secondly, and most seriously, there is the Sunderland debacle. Mick clearly wanted the job. The rags had him odds on. But no approach was ever made. 'We think you're wonderful,' all England is telling him, 'but we wouldn't dream of employing you.' Mick's openness to offers reeks of desperation. He stands on the sideline in his FAI tracksuit, looking like the last remaining item in a bomb sale.

As we always do, we run at them to start with, huffing and puffing, on the off chance of an early goal. When none comes the game, the ground, and the pub in which we're watching all descend into an odd lull. It's awful. It would hurt to see the team prove it can cope without Roy, but not half as much as it hurts to see Ireland being out-passed by Switzerland's finest. In injury time of the first half they launch it from the near side of the centre circle to the far post, where some unknown is loitering to lob it back over Given's head into the empty net. Sky's presenter has a face like thunder, as if he means to say, 'We paid good money for this?'

'Of course,' my younger brother says to me during the ads, 'you've always been one of Mick's great apologists.'

This has been one of the summer's comic refrains. We clutched elimination from the jaws of qualification two tournaments on the trot. Any other nation in Europe would have had Mick's head on a spike in the capital long before now. But our collective self-congratulatory decency, our innate against-all-odds amateurism, insisted that sacking managers was poor form. And spokesman for the defence? Muggins here, the thesis being that Mick was *unlucky*. Now even Mick thinks he's unlucky. It's written all over his face in the second half. You could be forgiven for imagining that Player Cam is currently following the Irish manager. He stands in the restriction zone, a step ahead of all the others, hands behind his back and, as he says himself, his chin up and his chest out. His posture speaks pride but his face says, 'What a flippin' way to go!'

Then we score. A scramble on their 6-yard line that gets latched on to by our centre-half, Gary Breen – 1–1 and Landsdowne Road is heaving. The left back, Ian Harte, makes way for Gary Doherty. A few near misses and the clock runs down. Just when the whole pub is beginning to wonder whether or not another moral victory will be enough to save Mick's bacon, the Swiss break through the old inside-right channel. Given dives and it looks as if it has gone wide. But the silence, however momentary, is such that you can actually hear the leather catching the slackened net, Celestini's yelp of disbelief. I ask, 'A goal?'

'A goal.'

Then, in injury time, the first faint echoes of 'Keano-o, Keano-o . . .' There is no groundswell. The echoes are more like an old favourite number being played on a stereo in an adjoining flat. You can't quite hear the tune or the words, but you can make out enough of a muffle to reconstruct the rest from memory. The echoes diminish for an instant, return with fractionally greater anger. One of the regulars beneath the telly cranks up the volume with the zapper. A handful of punters row in, laughing.

'KEANO-O, KEANO-O . . .'

'Oh fuck,' the barman chortles. 'There'll be sport now.'

The seconds are running out. The producer goes back to Mick and holds. Goaded by a backdrop that choruses the name of his old adversary, he looks desperate to remain unbowed. But he can't resist. Just before the whistle, he flinches. Perhaps even 'flinch' is too much. It's more an involuntary backward glance into the stands. In cricket they say no batsman who has been clean bowled can resist a retrospective peek at his splattered stumps. What does Mick see over his shoulder? A galaxy of faces mooning back at him, helpless to know what to think or do. The ref flaps his arms. There is a flurry of handshakes, a smattering of applause and barracking as the team disappears into the tunnel, the solemn faces of the pundits like mourners at a funeral. We leave by the front door. As we do so, two old flames on high stools in the front bar are serenading one another with the Neil Diamond/Barbara Streisand classic 'You Don't Bring Me Flowers Anymore'. Goodnight.

Next day, a good week shy of needing a trim, I drop in on Benny. Swaddled in wraps and towels, I say, 'Switzerland, Benny.'

'Yeah, Switzerland.'

'Starting to look like a bad *month* at the office.'

'Macedonia, Wales . . .'

'Yeah?'

Wales beat Italy at home, and Macedonia took a very creditable point away to England. Benny is seriously suggesting that there was some sort of unfavourable planetary alignment last night, or just a plain old underdogs' moon. Me and half the country have suffered through the guts of six months. Now that the tide is turning I am not letting go.

'Ah but Switzerland, Benny. *Swit-zer-land.*'

'Yeah.'

The way he says it you can tell this is no longer idle slagging between lads. This is agony. He says nothing for the rest of the ride. Nothing, except a curt 'Thanks now'. So I don't push it. I just go.

70

A house of cards. The FAI says they will not sack Mick, and yet by the last week of October they are reported to be scouting the continent for a replacement. On Tuesday, 5 November Mick arrives to dine with FAI officials in Kilkea Castle, Athy. He has agreed, in principle, to step down but wishes to explain his reasons personally. He and his agent, Liam Gaskin, are on the Naas dual carriageway when news comes on the radio of his impending resignation. Gaskin calls the FAI and asks to reschedule their meeting for 8pm in Merrion Square. Mick sits alone upstairs while a severance deal is negotiated on his behalf. There is a press conference in the Burlington Hotel at 9pm, in time for the main evening news. Tommy and me watch it on the edge of the coffee table, just like old times.

Mick: 'I feel immense pride. It has been a privilege.'

Tommy: 'What's a privilege?'

Me: 'An honour, something you're lucky to have a chance to do.'

Mick: 'This is what I do. This is what I enjoy doing.'

Tommy: 'Giving interviews?'

Me: 'Managing.'

Tommy: 'But he isn't the manager any more.'

Never speak ill of the dead, they say. Suffering pangs of guilt over pints the following night, we compile a verbal inventory entitled 'Good Things About Mick'. There is some hesitation as to who will get the ball rolling. We snigger, wipe our smiling faces, knuckle down to the task. He was a decent centre-half in his day, an effective Irish captain. He had the guts to change the stone-age style of play patented by his mentor. He blooded gifted youngsters before they realised how difficult international football could be. He eked the most out of bit-part players who would never have been considered by other countries. He got the only world-class Irish footballer of this generation on the pitch in green for kick-off, despite that footballer's initial disenchantment with the team and its chances. We pause. He had a smashing head of hair. We snigger some more. He did the decent thing.

What did that pause contain? A summer's worth of recrimination, if truth be told. So many hypotheses have been have been put forward as to Roy's state of mind in Saipan. What about Mick's? He must have known, long before they touched down in Saipan, who was given the credit for their qualification. 'If there was any doubt that everybody in Ireland knows this,' Fintan O'Toole wrote on 24 May, 'it was banished by the radio phone-in shows yesterday as the news from Saipan was greeted as a national disaster.' Did that knowledge play on his mind? He certainly seemed to lose sight of the terms of his employment. 'It became apparent that he didn't see it as his job to put the best Irish team possible on the pitch,' Tom Humphries writes in today's *Irish Times*, 'but to get the best possible out of those he put on the pitch.' Once that shift of emphasis took place in Mick's head, his days were numbered.

That weekend Happy Niall announces his retirement from football. Period. He walks the pitch of the Stadium of Light before the league game against Spurs to a standing ovation, and presents a giant cheque for kids' charities in Sunderland and Dublin. A week after Mick's resignation the Genesis Report arrives, named after an independent Glasgow consultancy firm that canvassed opinions on Ireland's World Cup furore. The report is not published in full and the findings that are released are decidedly tame. Much of the criticism of the FAI is general to the association's power structures. Saipan? Nobody told Roy it was meant to be fun, the gear should have been there on time and there was no crisis management procedure in place. Apart from that, it was top notch. In spite of such tepid criticisms, the General Secretary Brendan Menton is forced to resign. After his resignation, Menton writes a formal letter to the officers of the association questioning an 'exceptional payment' of £100,000 made to McCarthy. The sum was based on a verbal agreement struck between Mick and the association treasurer, John Delaney, in a hotel bedroom in Chiba in the wee hours immediately after our 1–1 win over Germany.

Two days after Mick's resignation Roy flies into Cork to honour a book-signing at Easons that was rescheduled after his hip operation. The autograph hunters are so numerous that crash barriers have to be erected and a Garda unit is present. 'Keano-o, Keano-o' rings out all over the city centre and the branch sells over a thousand copies. It is on the main evening news. In response to the inevitable question about his international future, he is reported to have told one fan, 'If they get a good manager.'

Jason McAteer goes on talkSport's *No Nonsense Sports Breakfast* and urges his old adversary to make a comeback. 'After all that has gone on between us, I do actually like Roy,' he says. Robbie Keane says much the same on Radio 5 Live and Clinton Morrison tells

BBC Sport that 'all the players want him back.' Mindful of the speculation, Sir Alex publicly silences his captain. 'I think for Roy's sake, the least he says about it the better,' he says. Sir Alex omits, however, to muzzle the other current Irish Red Devil, John O'Shea. John wasn't in the squad for the World Cup. He was only just breaking into the United team and Mick, he reckons, never came to watch him. John couldn't walk down the street for people asking him whether or not the latest Roy rumours were true. Speaking in Athens in the third week of November before Ireland's friendly, John tells reporters, 'I hope Roy comes back and I think he will.'

71

The swimming recommences on Wednesday, 13 November. The night before, after the kids have gone to bed, my wife goes rummaging through the shelves under the stairs for our beach bag. We bought it at Carnac-Plages two years ago. We have kept all togs and towels and armbands in it ever since. I am filling the insurance disclaimer on the kitchen table when I hear her laughing, 'Well what d'ya know!'

'Surprise me,' I say through the open door. 'What do I know?'

She says nothing. Instead a decidedly damp, chlorine-scented, hand-held Mr Roy Keane peers around the architrave. He has been wrapped in Tommy's tricolour beach towel since the second last day of July, reeking of Mediterranean sea salt. There are even patches of blue mould on his green jersey, and his woollen boot laces have come undone. After her own initial delight subsides, mine proves too prolonged.

'Jesus,' she says, 'would that we all got such a welcome!'

'Tommy'll be thrilled. I'll go up and tell him.'

'He's out of it.'

'This guy could use a bath.'

I fill the sink in the downstairs loo with lukewarm water, pop three drops of my wife's lavender oil in on the sly and leave him to soak. Back early from the pub, I tuck him in under the lagging jacket on the cylinder. As I am brushing my teeth in the en suite, it hits me. Between rinses I say to my semi-comatose wife in the next room, 'If you think about it . . .'

'I know,' she groans. 'I feel a metaphor coming on.'

'Even you have to admit it's a bit spooky.'

'Enough said.'

'His going missing coincides with Roy's period in the wilderness. And now, a week after Mick retires . . .'

'. . . he reappears, wrapped in the tricolour. Subtle.'

'Be like that.'

In the morning, I have him propped up against Tommy's Weetabix bowl before the kids are dressed. I tell Tommy on the landing to expect a surprise. He goes down in one sock and his underwhelmed 'Ah brilliant' is clearly designed for his old man's ears. I ask him if he'd like to take Mr Roy Keane in to school and he declines. When I go to the pool to collect them, however, I leave Mr Roy Keane on Tommy's side of the back seat and Tommy, T-shirt inside out and hair scrambled, seems genuinely glad.

72

You got a lotta nerve to say you are my friend
When I was down you just stood there grinning
You got a lotta nerve to say you got a helping hand to lend
You just want to be on the side that's winning.

Bob Dylan, 'Positively 4th Street'

183

When Mick McCarthy took over from Jack Charlton as manager the national anthem was the last thing on his mind. Then, so the story goes, he received a parcel in the post from a member of the public. The accompanying letter expressed the writer's disappointment at the sight of members of an Irish team facing the tricolour tight-lipped. Mick found enclosed an instructional video on how to sing 'Amhránn na bhFiann' ('The Soldiers' Song') and the Gaelic lyrics written out phonetically. At the earliest opportunity, Mick assembled the team into one of the back rooms and got them to sing it together from scratch. The Irish among them could neither remember the air nor translate the words. To the English-born players it was gibberish. Mick told them to learn it. So they did, and sang it before every game.

Except Roy. Roy never seemed to sing a note, and there were lots of nights when he was the only one. 'The pre-match ceremonial bullshit,' he calls it in another context. There is one great shot of the team singing the anthem before the home tie with Holland, looking up the line from halfway down. All the players to Shay Given are obviously singing. They have been caught in the middle of some broad vowel, like a nest of cuckoos waiting for their mother to drop a worm. Roy, last man at the back, is biting his lower lip. His half-shut eyes are turned up to the heavens. He could be lost in the melody, or trying to block it out, or just as easily thinking 'Get me out of here!'

It's clear that over the years of his international career he grew to associate singing with a version of Irishness he found increasingly difficult to tolerate. Remembering the trip on the team bus to play Italy in New York in 1994, he pokes fun at the multiple ironies inherent in the rebel songs being blasted out on the tape recorder. On one hand there are the corny simplistic songs themselves and their 'stories of English oppression and how our Irish heroes fought gallantly'. On the other hand there is the altogether deeper irony in the fact that Cockney and Scouse lads in the squad 'sang as lustily as the rest'. In the interview he gives to Sean O'Hagan for the *Observer*, his sarcasm is palpable: 'The good old Irish, we'll just have a singsong if we're beaten.'

Roy, along with the rest of the squad, was smiling and clapping and singing to the resident band in the ballroom of the Saipan Hyatt when Mick appeared at the door. Mick called a halt to the festivities just as the band was launching into their cover of 'Stand By Me'. Roy, Niall Quinn, Jason McAteer and Steve Finnan were at the one table. Jason gave Niall a nudge and whispered that he wondered if Roy would still be singing by the time the meeting was over. According to Philip Quinn's version in the *Irish Independent* of the next morning, Roy left the room after his ten-minute, full-throttle tirade 'to the surreal accompaniment of the house band playing Herb Alpert's "The Girl from Ipanema"'.

On the bus from the hotel to the airport the next morning, the team was singing again. Mick Byrne, assistant physio, warmed them up with the theme song of one of the tots' programmes on TV he watched with his recently born first grandchild. Before long they were in fine voice. McCarthy, as ever unable to eschew the less than subtle message, says they sang 'We're on the One Road'. On Wednesday, 28 May, the night after Roy's decision not to return, Mick went to a bar in Izumo for a few beers and someone played U2's 'With or Without You' on the jukebox for devilment. Damien Duff's brother took his guitar to the all-night session in Ibaraki after our 1–1 win over Germany. Damien sang 'Leroy Brown', Robbie Keane did his usual showstopper 'Joxer Goes to Stuttgart' and Niall sailed close to shore with the folk standard 'The Ferryman'. Three weeks later Gary Kelly injured himself with a microphone during 'Mustang Sally' in a karaoke bar in Seoul. He wore a baseball cap to training the next afternoon and was revived by Mick Byrne's magic sponge. At the homecoming party in Phoenix Park on 18 June, Shay Given persuaded 100,000 fans to join him in serenading Jason with 'Happy Birthday'. 'That's our way,' Niall wrote in his tournament diary for the *Irish Independent*, 'the Irish way.'

All of which excludes the ex-captain, but for one intriguing detail. In his drinking days, Roy's party piece on nights out with the Ireland squad was a rendition of Bob Dylan's 'Positively 4th Street'. Sounds hard to believe, but several separate references attest to his credentials as a Dylan-head. He told Paul Kimmage that his CD trove included 'a bit of Bob Dylan'. When the trio of journalists knocked on the door of his room in the Saipan Hyatt, the morning he was due to fly home, they could hear Dylan's nasal whine inside. A further more definite story occurs in Niall's autobiography. The occasion was the night after the draw at home with Portugal, as recently as the beginning of June 2001. Roy had scored that day and generally played out of his skin. Everyone said so, even the Portuguese. Niall says it was the first night in years he had gone out with them:

> We wound up in the piano bar in Lillie's Bordello. Roy was wonderful company. He gave his shirt to a fan. He got up and sang Bob Dylan. He chatted and cracked jokes. Peter Reid was there and I remember him saying to me, 'Isn't Roy Keane a great guy.'

The image is entirely at odds with the one we always had of him. He never struck you as one of life's warblers. It wasn't until the fateful interview for the *Irish Times* that most of us became aware that there was ever a period in Roy's life you could have classed his 'singing days'. Tom Humphries, cuter than most journalists by a country mile, raised it out of nowhere:

'What's that song you've been heard to sing,' Tom asked, ' "Positively 4th Street"?'

Initially, Roy wasn't playing ball.

'My singing days are over,' he said. 'How does that one go again?'

Tom jogged his memory with some of the lyrics. The interview appeared in Q&A format. In the absence of notation, we have to guess. But I think it is a safe guess that in this exchange they were both smiling.

'Oh yeah,' Roy finally owned up, 'that one. In my defence, I was only joining in.'

Did any of his team-mates join in as well? Not, you imagine, if they paid any attention to the lyrics. The song, believed to address the Baez sisters and Dylan's Greenwich Village phase in general, is a pretty bitter valediction. It has been said that the other players always wondered what their skipper thought of them, that they found out for the first time in Saipan. Roy could argue that he had already spelled it out, but it seems not to have registered.

Except with Mick. There is no evidence that Mick was present that night in Lillie's Bordello, apart from something he said at his resignation press conference in the Burlington Hotel, something echoing a verse towards the end of 'Positively 4th Street':

And though I know you're dissatisfied with your position and
    your place
Don't you understand it's not my problem.

One voice from the floor asked Mick what he thought would happen with the Roy Keane situation. For six years Mick had sat in the band room under Landsdowne Road and expressed his disappointment at the negative line of questioning. Now here he was, looking like a man being forced to suck a slice of particularly unripe lemon one last time. He heaved a long impatient sigh, then sat back and smiled. Something had come back to him: 'Do you know what,' he said, 'it's not my problem.'

73

The third week of November and the new young woman invites me to her seat. I stay put, indicate that I'll wait for Benny. He usually prides himself on the speed of his dry cuts. Today, it's snail's pace. When he finishes the man ahead of me, he disappears out the back, ostensibly for a slash. I can hear the taps, the hand dryer humming twice. I am on the spot when he returns.

We say nothing. I keep smiling at him in the mirror, and Benny focuses on the job. I am playing the archetypal stirrer, something at which I am alarmingly good. Benny confines himself to dry, petulant, throat-clearing coughs. I start whistling.

'Happy man, huh? Happy man.'

'Life's good. You know yourself, Benny.'

If we were out the back, he would have thrown a haymaker my way by now. But we both know this is his bread and butter and the row of faces on the bench are watching him. I am pushing it farther than I ordinarily would. His face is simmering a deepish shade of pink.

'You should be ashamed of yourself,' he says.

'How do you work that one out?'

'Best manager we ever had.'

'Oh, a genius.'

'You all should be ashamed of yourselves, that's all I'll say. A great Irishman, hounded out of his job.'

'Look on the bright side, Benny.'

'What *bright side*?'

'The boy wonder can come back.'

'He's a tramp, a knacker.'

'You need to read your Bible a bit more.'

'What *Bible?*'

'The parable of the prodigal son. The good son and the playboy? The fatted calf? Ring any bells?'

A couple of the heads on the bench start laughing. I get my jacket and, out of pure badness, shove my face close to his.

'Head high, Benny. Chin up. Chest out. Rejoice for he was lost and now is found.'

'Fuck off.'

74

The night after that injury-time horror show in Macedonia, Mick sat on his own in a room in a Skopje hotel watching *Lethal Weapon*. Tony Cascarino compares the team's journey to the play-off in Bursa a month later with the Steve Martin comedy *Planes, Trains & Automobiles*. Roy missed 'A Night With Niall' to go to the pictures with his wife, but doesn't say what they saw. On the flight from Amsterdam to Tokyo he was glued to Will Smith as *Ali*, a movie he claims had a huge influence on his thinking. On the afternoon of 22 May, the rest day Wednesday in Saipan, while Roy was signing his death warrants with Paul Kimmage and Tom Humphries, and half the squad played golf, another splinter group went to a matinee of the *Star Wars* sequel, *Attack of the Clones*. On the Guam–London leg of his flight home two days later, Roy sat distractedly through *Training Day* starring Denzel Washington. Throughout the World Cup Mick's mobile phone rang to the theme tune of *Mission Impossible*.

There is one other film that has yet to hit your screens. It is, of course, the biopic, the story of Roy's fall and rise simplified for celluloid. In the *Daily Telegraph* of 24 May, the day after the final banishment, Henry Winter claimed that 'one of the world's most respected production companies is making a film of Keane's life.' Winter may well be privy to something about which the rest of us are in the dark. He even went so far as to suggest a side-splitting title: *Postcards from the Edge*. True or not, the idea is at least worthy of conjure. It has all the ingredients Hollywood needs: the individual's realisation of a dream by force of will, struggling against prejudice and his own limitations; public adulation, private torment and partial dressing-room nudity; a covert Republican tract, one nation struggling from the shadow of another in the quest for truth.

Coming shortly to a cinema near you . . . *BALLS*, a Neil Jordan/ Buena Vista 'based on a true story' blockbuster. Roy will be played by Colin 'Seven Million Dollars a Movie' Farrell, his head shaved and his *Tigerland* autopilot Nam private (complete with dog tags) reprised on the killing fields of Saipan. Mick will be given the Charles Dance treatment, the archetypal public-school baddie bristling malevolent Englishness, the suspicion of a cravat lurking beneath his tracksuit and a cricket bat permanently in his hand:

'Either you come over for this friendly against the Soviet Union, Keane, or I shall personally see to it that you never play for Southern Ireland again.'

A host of our finest thespians will be reduced to hamming it up in flat caps and composite bit parts. Russell Crowe will drift in and out, spouting Patrick Kavanagh, as the hero's unnamed ghost. Daniel Day Lewis will spend a winter in the pubs and on the hurling pitches of Crumlin researching his cameo as Niall Quinn, for which he will be awarded a BAFTA as best supporting male:

'Roy, think of all the sick kids who'll never have a chance to play in a World Cup. We've gotta make this thing work for their sake.'

It will be the major motion picture of the summer. The trailer will run for months in advance, its husky Marlboro Man voiceover proclaiming 'the story of one man who loved his country more than his country loved him'. A soundtrack featuring all of Ireland's leading recording artists will go on sale. Roy and Theresa will be guests of honour at the all-star black-tie premiere. They will be interviewed on the steps of the Savoy for the main evening news, flanked by Bono and Bertie Ahern. The broadsheets will herald another new dawn of Irish cinema and trip, as usual, over their superlatives.

Cork in the seventies will look suspiciously like Sheffield in the Great Depression. Roy will travel to Dublin in a jarvey for the game that would change his life. Just has they arrive in Fairview Park, he'll ask, 'Will I ever get the chance to prove my worth?' and the coach will answer, 'Sure faith who knows, Roy Boy, today might be the day you've dreamed of all your life.' Brian Clough will be played by Pete Postlethwaite. The walls of the Anfield visitors' dressing room will be red brick and dripping condensation so the folks back in Nebraska know this is working-class England:

'Irishman, what the flippin' heck does thou think thou's playin' at? Get th'number seven shirt on thy back. Thou's playin' thy first game in the British League this very night against the mighty Liverpool.'

There will be a long montage, to the backdrop of U2's 'Pride (In the Name of Love)', that takes us all the way from the City ground to Dublin Airport in May 2002 via Turin and Barcelona. The conclusion will hinge on a fuzzy conspiracy theory, hinting at collusion between the FAI and MI5. The team meeting will be billed as a showdown, the OK Corral of Irish football. Mick will be smirking,

'The FAI let me down about the balls.'

'You *are* the FAI, McCarthy. You're the problem.'

'If you leave this restaurant, Keane, then you're never coming back.'

'Don't worry, I don't want back. You can stick this World Cup up your ass, you English son-of-a-bitch.'

Roy packing his bags, arriving in Heathrow and disappearing into the Cheshire sunset with his golden retriever will be played out under mystical synthesisers and Sinead O'Connor howling 'The Fields of Athenry' in her customary banshee *sean nós*. A paragraph of closing text will explain about the Genesis Report and Mick's resignation. Then the credits will roll.

75

Our jerseys are hanging on pegs – one to five, then seven to twenty-three.

Niall Quinn, *Niall Quinn: The Autobiography*

In those blank three or four months over Christmas, when we have no manager and no matches and no points, I wonder about Roy's jerseys designed especially for Korea/Japan. Roy probably didn't care what happened to them, and still doesn't. He gave every scrap of his official FAI/Umbro training and casual wear to the cleaners of the Saipan Hyatt on the morning of his premature departure:

I said to them to take them. I left quite a bit there. No point in bringing them back. Left my shoes there with the Irish flag on the back. I'd say somebody is playing football in them, only there's no football pitches in Saipan.

Every player gets a monograph version for every international, competitive or friendly. This, along with the national anthem, was another of Mick's initiatives. There is the FAI crest, the Umbro logo, and then vertically down the breastbone in between are the player's number, the fixture details and the date. What happened to Roy's? Where did they go? Who got them, and what did they do with them?

Tommy wants an official Ireland jersey for Christmas. We

bought an Ireland jersey of sorts for his birthday at the beginning of May, with the World Cup just around the corner. We figured €50 for an official jersey was too much and bought in a department store. It was grand. Granted, the shade of green was too emerald to be true. It had an incorrect v-neck and the orange of its trimmings was troublingly red. To add to the Italian undertones, the 'brand name' was one neither of us had ever heard of, and the longer you muttered the word the more its cod continental gloss wore off: *Futti*.

Tommy couldn't believe his luck. He wore it day and night. Before and after Ireland matches he ran to the end of the close and back in his Ireland top, his Tesco tricolour billowing on its bamboo pole behind him and Eve bringing up the rear on her Barbie bike. When it got smelly, my wife lifted it from the back of the chair in their room while they slept and put it in the wash. For two days of every week, Tommy sulked in his unofficial Brazil jersey. Then he wore it to the screening of the Germany game at school and the first thing he asked when he got into the car at half two was, 'Dad, is my jersey "official"?'

I tried to stall him, to sing dumb.

' "Official"? I'd say so.'

'One of the other boys said his jersey was "official" and mine was a cheapo job.'

'Sure, it says Ireland on it, doesn't it?'

'Yeah . . .'

'Well, there you go.'

He wore it less after the tournament had finished. Deep into August, well after we got back, he wore it to a friend's house. The friend's dad had bought in a different department store. Theirs was crewneck, closer to the mark. It had that silky sheen that felt official, whereas Tommy's had a distinctly aertex touch to the fingertips. But it had an unignorable lime hue and it had a crest that looked like a badge you got off a birthday card. They recognised that they were both wearing Ireland jerseys, but that their Ireland jerseys looked nothing like each other. What began as a squabble as to whose was the real McCoy concluded as a mutual conviction that they had both been conned.

In September, Tommy started going to football every Saturday morning with two of his pals. I took it upon myself as a father–son bonding thing. I drove them at half nine, and sat with a flask of Nescafé and the papers while the lads got put through their paces. Every Friday night he laid out his chosen kit for the next day, and was there beside the bed at the crack of dawn in his shin guards and studs, saying, 'Dad, c'mon.'

One week it was Liverpool. There was never an issue about getting him that official jersey. That was a natural rite of passage, a moment to fight back the tears. Another week it was the azure of the Italia jersey his granny brought back from Sirmione, or the canary of Brazil. It gradually came to my attention that it was never the Irish green. Initially, I thought he had just gone as lukewarm on the national squad as the rest of us. I was wrong.

He says he wants the official Ireland jersey for Christmas. So one afternoon in early December, while the pair are at a birthday party, I wander along to the local branch of a renowned sports franchise and talk the talk. Since Mick has taken the jump, the idea of subscribing to FAI merchandise sticks less in my throat. Also, I am in luck. A combination of variables – the fact Ireland are suddenly struggling and the imminent arrival of a whole new strip – has meant that the old ones in stock are being flogged at a substantial reduction. The assistant shows me the official stamp and we discuss washing temperatures. I ask, 'Do you recommend Surf Automatic?'

'Sorry?'

'Forget it.'

While my Visa card is being swiped I remember that Tommy requested a name and number on the back. The assistant says they don't print names and numbers, but that a smaller private shop two streets away does. Laughing slightly, he asks as if he already knows the answer, 'Any particular name and number?'

I can't help myself.

'Keane, six.'

He laughs some more and shakes his head as well. I think he is taking the piss.

'What?'

'Nothing,' he says holding his hands up in surrender. 'Nothing. I can't talk about it. Company policy.'

'It's company policy that staff don't engage in conversation with customers about Roy and Mick and Saipan?'

'Got it in one.'

'That's mad.'

'Too many rows, mate, far too many rows in the shop. I can see how it sounds mad to you on the outside, but believe me it's a relief to us in here.'

The smaller private shop is manned by a gauche teenager with a complexion like pizza. I say my piece and he begs twenty minutes to get it done. I am halfway across the street to try on expensive clothes I have no intention of buying when I begin to doubt if I said the right number. It's a bit like lying down in bed and forgetting whether or not you flicked off the wall switch on the telly. I step back in.

'I did say "Keane, ten", didn't I? I didn't say "Keane, six"?'

'It's ten.'

'Grand.'

'Is that what you want?'

'Absolutely.'

I don't usually use *absolutely* as an affirmative, but this time I suppose I want to be emphatic, simply to avoid confusion. He misinterprets the emphasis and says, 'Not the other cunt!'

It's an odd moment. I feel sorry for the lad. I think he was saying only what he thought I wanted to hear.

'No,' I mumble and go up the road.

The letters and figures are still hot when I collect them. I pay €9 and neither of us meets the other's eye. Tommy feigns surprise with aplomb, gasps 'Aw cool . . .' and wears his official jersey all of Christmas morning. The first Saturday of the New Year I drop him and his pals off. The under-sixes' hour is just wrapping up. They come off to their mams and dads. Tommy chases his Champions' League ball onto the indoor pitch as if the indoor pitch were Landsdowne Road on a big Wednesday night. I go down to the sea front to read the papers and kill three-quarters of an hour. I arrive back in time to hear the echoes of 'Keano-o, Keano-o' coming down the corridor and don't need to be told who has just scored.

76

The most interesting vignette in Mick's book describes a lift ride with Roy in the Saipan Hyatt on Monday, 20 May. It was lunchtime and Mick, dashing across the lobby, called for the door to be held. He made it, just, and found his skipper inside, smiling mischievously and saying that he was actually trying to shut it before Mick got in.

'You would and all,' Mick says he said.

Roy had gone to Mick's room on Saturday night to have his say in private about the absent kit. Both testify to that. At the time, however, several reports suggested that Mick had repaid the courtesy immediately after the ballroom blowout, to issue a formal banishment. That seems not to have happened. On the evidence we have, this remains their last one-to-one. The infamous skips had washed up in the wee hours and Roy was togged out for the first time in his official Umbro gear. That Mick complimented him on his appearance suggests a conversation that wasn't roaring. Mick, however, found his voice just as the bell was dinging:

> As I leave the lift I tell him that I hope he stands in my shoes one day and gets the chance to manage a team.

Mick should take comfort from the news that the bookies are at least offering odds on Roy as his replacement. Paddy Power have him as an 80–1 outsider, neck and neck with Sven Goran Eriksson. Odds of 500–1 are also being offered on Eamon Dunphy with Roy as his Ian Evans. Even before Mick wandered into the night, Johnny Giles was making a case for Keane as player-manager. Within weeks of the race commencing, Bryan Robson is being hotly tipped, and the *Irish Examiner* claims that he has already proposed Roy as his sidekick. Deposed Sunderland boss Peter Reid, with Niall Quinn upstairs, is the diplomatic alternative. The clear early favourite, however, is John Toshack based solely on the fact that he was spotted in Dublin the day Mick resigned.

Apart from Roy, other former Irish internationals in with a shout are Joe Kinnear (2–1), John Aldridge (7–2), Ronnie Whelan (14–1), Niall *tout seul* (33–1) and Denis Irwin (100–1). Two old favourites who stall at the first fence are David O'Leary and Liam Brady. O'Leary, still between jobs after his sudden exit from Leeds, wants the job but not while he is still in the full of his health. Brady, who nailed his colours firmly to Mick's mast during Saipan, is altogether more scathing. Because things were a mess in his day, so they should remain. He tells the *Cork Evening Echo*:

> The criteria is [sic] to reconcile Roy Keane, and I wouldn't bother. The media has given Keane totally unacceptable power. What's it going to take the next time? Is it going to be the fact that the pasta is not right? There's lots of very, very fine players

who have played for Ireland and had to put up with some of the things Roy Keane has had to put up with.

In early December former Northern Ireland boss Brian Hamilton is contracted to canvass candidates. After speaking to about twenty possibilities, Hamilton presents a shortlist of six in the second week of January. Although oddly cloak-and-dagger, the shortlist is believed to include Kenny Dalgliesh; Bryan Robson; Peter Reid; Kevin Moran; Bernard Troussier, the Frenchman who managed Japan in the World Cup; and Brian Kerr, FAI director of football. All the others put their cases. On Monday the 27th the news that Kerr will be formally unveiled as manager appears by accident on the FAI website. Two days later the press assemble in the Shelbourne Hotel and Kerr calls himself 'somebody ordinary who is trying to achieve something extraordinary'. It all happens in such haste that someone forgets to write 'Dear John' letters to the other applicants.

Was the job always Kerr's? There is no doubt that he is the overwhelming popular choice. His achievements managing the Republic of Ireland youth teams – third in the World Youth Championships in Malaysia in 1997 with the U-20 team, winners of the U-16 European Championships in Scotland in 1998 – means he is already the most successful Irish manager ever. Even more interesting than his careers stats is his history with his two immediate predecessors. He had been a coach with the Irish Youth team from 1982 to 1986. Then, in 1986, the new senior manager, Jack Charlton, famously barged into the dressing room at half-time in a Youth international against England and took over the team talk. Liam Tuohy, the then Youth manager, felt undermined and resigned. Kerr and his right-hand man, Noel O'Reilly, did too. Kerr was recalled after Jack's own resignation a decade later. After his team beat Italy in the Euro 1998 final, Mick griped: 'I don't think he ever said he wants my job but every time he wins something he's allegedly after my job.'

And Roy Keane? 'I want the best players to play for us,' Kerr says. He says he has a plan and leaves it at that. Roy is so up to speed on developments that it is he who tells John O'Shea, one of Kerr's class of 1998, of the appointment on the training ground later that week. John remembers:

I said I thought he would be a great manager for Ireland and Roy just gave me one of his smiles. We'll know soon enough what that smile meant.

77

In mid-January, I win a spot prize in a pub quiz. It's towards the end of the night. I have had a few jars – not enough to choose a Bailey's gift set, but enough to cheat someone else out of the prize. The ticket actually drawn is red number seven. I have red number eighty-seven, but cover the eight with the index finger on my left hand and shout 'Yes!' I get a round of applause, the quizmaster forgets to request my ticket and whoever has the real red number seven is either dozing or is too busy in the jacks bitching about the severity of the questions.

All the good spot prizes have been taken. I am left to choose between the aforementioned beverage, a Poundstretcher golf umbrella, a pair of matching figurine lamps and a video for kids. I despise Irish cream, my brother is a club pro who would never forgive me if I togged out with such tacky equipment and my wife insisted 'Not the bloody lamps'. The video it is: Dustin the Turkey in *Fowl Play*. I'm also swayed by the memory of the turkey voicing his support of Roy last May.

The blurb on the box promises a story of 'joy and heartbreak'. Tommy and Eve are not fussed. They leave the video in the video drawer for weeks. We go west for a long weekend at the beginning of February and my wife has the foresight to pack a few contingencies. Then two whole days on the trot are lost to that fine sideways rain in which the west of Ireland specialises. By teatime on Day Two we are down to Dustin. I'm eating toast when Tommy starts shouting,

'Dad, Niall Quinn's in it.'

'Oh yeah.'

'Come in.'

'In a minute.'

I don't. In fact, I forget all about it until bedtime. Overseeing the brushing of teeth, I ask if the video was any good. Tommy says it was crap but that Niall Quinn's in it. This time it registers, without any credible interest. They rinse. When Tommy spits and surfaces for air, he says, 'And guess what, Dad.'

'What?'

'He's the baddie.'

'Dustin?'

'No, Niall.'

'*Niall?*'

He mimics my tone.

'Yeah, *Niall*. He's the bad guy.'

Intrigued, I watch it after my wife hits the sack. Dustin is a cowboy builder in Dublin, aided and abetted by Snotser the Pig. We join the action just as they are finishing a dodgy renovation of Niall's house. We don't see Niall, but Dustin and Snotser agree that they would have thought a footballer like Niall Quinn could afford a house in a better area and better builders. A window falls out on the last syllable of 'builders', they leg it and we hear Niall's unmistakeable voice barking from indoors, 'Come back here ya rotten little turkey.'

Dustin, disillusioned, resolves to emulate Louis Walsh and become a millionaire with his new boyband, Mankind. He holds auditions and assembles five gormless, sweet-voiced lads. Lurking in the shadows, however, is the mysterious Mr Strange. The 'action' culminates with a showdown in a classroom-cum-studio (it says STUDIO at the door, but it also has a blackboard). In a final desperate bid to take over Mankind, Mr Strange reveals his true identity. It was Niall, you kind of realised, all along. Nine months after his retirement from international football, Niall is still sporting the green jersey.

'Quinner, so you're the bad guy,' Dustin howls. 'But you can't be. You're the Mother Teresa of Irish football.'

'Correction. I *was* the Mother Teresa of Irish football. There's no more Mr Nice Guy.'

You scarcely need me to point out the Saipan allegory. The unit is in danger of being sundered by a solitary malign force. There is even a slanging match (Niall calls Dustin 'a burping farting unwashed chancer'). There are a few wry references for the cognoscenti. The €1m Niall claims to have to launch the band is also the approximate figure advertised as the proceeds of his charity match. Just as Mankind are about to take Niall's offer, he tells them they'll be paid in washing powder tablets.

'We're going to stay with Dustin,' one member tells a horrified Niall.

'Thing is,' another chimes in, 'he's our manager and he believes in us.'

All of which makes Dustin the Turkey Mick McCarthy. Mick would certainly echo the sentiments parroted on his behalf.

'All I have to give you is my honesty,' Dustin says to the band's approval.

The allegory is not slanted entirely to one side. It was Dustin's slapdash professionalism that made Niall bad in the first place. Niall reminds him of the windows, 'Dustin, you're the one that made me bad.'

Taking the allegory on its terms, the band must be the Irish squad. Snotser the Pig is an amalgam of Taff and Packie Bonner.

Dustin's lowlife associates must be the FAI. And Niall, acting out his dark side, is Roy.

78

Teatime on 11 February, the Tuesday. I am sitting with my kids at the kitchen table when the call comes. They are eating mini pizzas and mine is a cheese sandwich. I am put in mind of the night before the Holland game in Rotterdam. I begin to tell them the significance of what we happen to be having and they scream, 'Here we go again!' My wife is already in the hall, and gets the phone on the second ring. She says my mother's name the way she always does, obviously glad it's her. Then her voice drops a notch.

'OK,' she says, 'I'll tell him.'

'Tell him what?' I call out with my mouth full of cheese sandwich in a way that makes the kids laugh.

'Roy Keane's on the telly,' she shouts back in.

'He's not coming back, is he?'

'No.'

It is the lead story on the six o'clock news, ahead of the Minister for Foreign Affairs' announcement that any action against Iraq would require a second UN resolution. The newscaster says that Michael Kennedy sent a statement to Tommy Gorman, the Belfast correspondent who did the interview last May, within the past hour. There is a report by Gorman, sketching the past year, and featuring footage of Roy walking his dog in lashing rain last June in which he has a saturated anorak and a flat cap that makes him look momentarily like Big Jack.

Tony O'Donoghue reports from Kilmarnock, where the Irish squad is training for tomorrow night's friendly. The announcement was made while Kerr was putting the team through its paces. Afterwards he spoke to a bouquet of mics and looked mightily pissed off. As far as Brian was concerned, he and Sir Alex had an agreement that the announcement would be withheld until Thursday. Then he talked about the players he still had at his disposal, about something called the future.

The same features appear on the nine o'clock news, the same faces and the same sentiments. The programme ends with a vox pop on the dark streets of Cork. 'A big loss' is the consensus, but there is no great surprise. Most recognise that Roy is getting on and that he has his young family to consider. Dunphy and Dervan spar one last time on the current affairs programme, *Primetime*, immediately after. They come across like ageing heavyweights in the interminable twelfth, leaning into one another and throwing tired aimless jabs. They are waiting for the bell. Dunphy was in the Christian Brothers in Tralee this morning, and the only question he was asked was would Roy be coming back. A player's first allegiance is to the people who pay his wages. He is, predictably, happy with the decision. Dervan, predictably, thinks Roy's timing stinks. He gets the last word, and thankfully it's a good one:

It's a very sad day for Roy Keane and Irish football. The only good thing to come out of this is that we now have closure on what has been a very traumatic twelve months for everybody. Mick McCarthy is no longer the Irish manager: Roy Keane had a big part to play in that. Roy Keane is no longer an international player.

79

When the hurlyburly's done,
When the battle's lost and won . . .

The following is witnessed by a friend of a friend called Tony. Tony is an actor currently touring the schools of the country with a production of *Macbeth*. He is one of the witches. On 14 February the company plays to 500 Leaving Cert students on a basketball court in Killarney, Co. Kerry. Despite the echoes, it goes down a bomb. By the time they get the make-up off and the set packed up, it is dark outside and there is bad news.

That evening Tony goes drinking in a bar in downtown Killarney with cast and crew. The talk is of nothing but Roy's retirement announcement. They play darts. Tony loses a game of five-o-one down, doubles to finish, to Banquo's Ghost and goes to buy a round. He is approached by one of two Corkmen. The barman does not like the look of them. He does not, especially, like the sound of their Rebel County accents. Would Tony order pints on their behalf? Tony, truth to tell, does not like the look of them either. But given the combination of their place of origin and the night that's in it, he doesn't feel as if he can say no.

A pint ordered on their behalf becomes three, becomes the remainder of the evening. Tony can't shake them off. The second Corkman is small, dark complexion, taciturn. He mopes in the margins, gazing at his pint swilling in his pint glass and shaking his head. The first is fairer, taller, talkative, cracks jokes to his own loudest laughs, hogs the darts, gets more competitive with every drink, and even questions the integrity of Lady Macbeth's subtraction when she beats him.

At closing time, just as everyone is making shapes, the second silent Corkman over in the corner starts groaning. They zip their anoraks as the groans grow into full-blown howls.

'Roy Keane,' the second Corkman is howling in a brogue you could slice and butter. 'Roy Keane. Best footballer in the world. Best footballer ever to play for Ireland. Fuckin' Mick McCarthy. Fuckin' Alex Ferguson. Bastards. Fuckin' bastards all of them.'

He puts his head in his hands and starts sobbing. The barman arrives, surprised the boys are still on the premises, and insists that this time they leave. The first Corkman carries both coats into the street while the second dries his eyes. The man, Tony says, was truly in mourning.

80

That Thursday Manchester City announces that it will not be taking Roy to court for his hatchet job on Alfie Haaland. The club had announced last August that its solicitors were compiling a case. At the time there were reports that Haaland had denied any connection between Roy's challenge and his injury on his own website, but the player's press statement was more ambiguous: 'I can only state that the period since that particular match has been difficult. I've never been fully fit since that episode.'

After four months' deliberation they have decided – given Alfie's career-threatening injury is on the other knee from the one Roy hit and the injury pre-dated April 2001 and he togged out both for City and Norway in the week after the tackle – 'that it would be difficult for Manchester City to take any action on medical grounds'. It is also announced the same day that Haaland has been served with six months' notice on his contract. Neither gets much column space.

I buy an armful of papers and Gerry says, 'You're a glutton for punishment.'

'Last time.'

We smile disconsolately. I go out of my way to pass Small World. I want to say something nasty about Sir Alex but haven't the guts when we come face to face. Small World is putting a brave spin on it.

'Great decision,' he says gazing at the base of his lollipop stick, 'great decision. Those FAI bastards dropped him like a bad penny last summer. Now that cry-baby McCarthy has been exposed for the bullshitter he is and the team needs a leg-up again, they come knocking on Keane's door.'

He's right, but his heart isn't behind the sentiments and neither is mine. Still, I agree for an easy life.

'Hypocrites,' he says. 'Fuckin' hypocrites.'

'Small world,' I say.

'Now you're talkin'!'

I get my hair cut that weekend. Me and Benny have what remains our last tête à tête on patriotism and the beautiful game. It's been a while. Not since my misquoted verse of the good book and his 'go forth and multiply' riposte have we broached this subject. It's bad.

'I hope you and your lot are happy,' he says when my head is half-shaved.

I try to sidestep this one, pleading bafflement.

'Happy about what?'

'You know,' he says.

'It's for the best.'

'Betrayed his country not once, but twice.'

'Benny,' I say, 'you didn't want him to come back. Now he's decided not coming back is for the best and you reckon he's a traitor all over again. Doesn't add up.'

'He should be shot like a dog.'

This is only the beginning. It concludes with your correspondent on his feet in a barber's cape. One of the other regulars attempts a conciliatory 'Fuck's sake lads', but there is no stopping us. Benny's tack is all tramps and pride in the jersey. He even gets in the hunger striker Bobby Sands. Mine is populated with the usual quota of 'yes-men' and blazers. We are at it hammer and tongs. With half my head shaved and the other not, I am a walking before-and-after shot. Benny has a live razor in his hand and is waving it beneath my downy nose for emphasis. We would be there yet, but for the words of Benny's boss: 'It's over.' They appear behind our own raised voices, like a dream that turns out to be someone shouting at the end of the bed, getting louder and louder.

'IT'S OVER!'

Silence. And then again, more quietly.

'It's over. Let it go.'

8 1

What really happened? The final newspaper tidal wave allows us to piece together the sequence of events with some accuracy.

On Thursday Kerr flew to Manchester. As far as he was concerned, only a few of his inner circle knew any of this was happening. That belief, however, was thrown by the sight of an RTÉ crew in situ to welcome him off the plane. Then, when he was in the cab on the way, he got a call on his mobile from a pal of Roy's with a message. There was already a posse of journalists and cameramen at the Marriott Hotel, waiting to catch his arrival. Roy's pal met Kerr's cab before it pulled into the car park, and then redirected them to another hotel where Roy was waiting.

They talked for three hours. It even sounds as if they talked Saipan openly, and what lay underneath that isolated evening. Kerr spoke of the FAI's commitment to change in the wake of Genesis. He accepted Roy's scepticism, but asked him to look at his record.

Roy had been one of the very few remaining players at senior level who didn't emerge out of Kerr's youth system, so hadn't first-hand experience. The smile meant the one thing none of us really expected. Roy was way beyond the point of persuasion. All he needed was to be asked. When they said goodbye Kerr felt he had been given an 'unequivocal commitment' to come back and play for Ireland. It was agreed he would be available to take up the reins again away to Georgia the following week.

Enter Sir Alex, a tad confused. Sir Alex had publicly expressed his hope the previous week that his captain would elect to concentrate on his club career and probably didn't expect to have to broach the subject again. Roy knew, going against the Gaffer's wishes, to pick his moment. So, after dropping his kids at school on Friday morning, he knocked on the office door and said his piece. Sir Alex was speechless. Can you blame him? Ferguson asked if he had spoken about the seriousness of his hip injury.

'Well,' Roy said, 'nah, not really.'

'Ferguson's annoyance was obvious,' David Walsh writes in the *Sunday Times* of 16 February, 'Keane's embarrassment equally so.' Word from the medical team was no less unequivocal. Play to a high standard for a couple of years with club only, or become yet another crock for club and country. Roy called Kerr the same day, Friday, and said what the doctor's orders were. Kerr asked him if it wasn't just a knee-jerk to scare stories told by people on the club payroll. Roy agreed to spend the weekend mulling it over.

He called Kerr again on Monday, said he was very impressed by what he saw and heard the previous Thursday, but that his mind hadn't budged an inch in the interim. Kerr accepted the sincerity of the decision, and they hung up on good terms. Roy called Michael Kennedy on Tuesday and they drafted a statement down the line. Kennedy spoke to Kerr's representative, Fintan Drury, who relayed the wish that the announcement be held back until Thursday, the day after the friendly with Scotland. Kennedy called Roy back to see what he thought. The previous day the *Irish Star* had run with the front-page headline: 'Keane Says YES'. Roy figured it was getting out of hand. 'No, let's do it now,' he said.

Fittingly, it ended as it began, in confusion and with a soupçon of bitterness. The statement went out on the main evening news. The Irish squad, at the time, was being put through its paces on the Hampden pitch in the rain. Kerr was called over into a huddle of tracksuits that included Packie Bonner. He looked confused. Someone handed him a mobile phone, he listened, spoke, signed off not looking best pleased and headed back towards the team. Later, at an impromptu press conference, he expressed his disappointment at the timing of the announcement. He finished by turning his and our attention to the remaining forty players 'who want to play for Ireland'.

Roy says he called Kerr again on Friday, wondering what that final aside was all about. Kerr said he was caught on the hop and generally regretted the way it went. Roy climbed down off his high horse, and they chatted for a bit. He didn't watch the friendly in Hampden. His daughters would probably have preferred it if he did. As it was, Ireland won 2–0 and the visiting fans sang, 'Are you watching, Roy Keane?'

No. I wasn't. I was at a parent teacher meeting at Shannon and Caragh's school . . . The reports were generally great, but like their dad they got that little comment, 'Could do better.'

82

An old school chum of my mother's stays overnight. They haven't seen each other in years and have a lot to catch up on. When the friend asks what the second youngest is up to at the moment, my mother tells her that I am writing a book and what the book is about.

'Don't mention that man's name, Joan, please,' the friend interrupts. 'We have an agreement in our house that we don't mention that person by name.'

My mother knows theirs was always a big Liverpool house. She also knows, however, that her own boys were always Liverpool too, but that for us Roy was immortal. And she figures that in her late fifties her friend shouldn't be so melodramatic. So my mother, the least confrontational person I have ever met, starts to say how sad the whole thing was, how sad the whole thing still is. The friend will not have it.

'Please Joan,' she keeps interrupting. 'I wish him luck with his book, but I don't want to talk about it.'

A week or so later I am travelling home on the evening commuter train from Dublin. The number of people travelling to and from the capital each day is escalating. I have to stand all the way. The driver pauses for a couple of minutes just as we are pulling into the platform. In that lull, I overhear a conversation between two jaded suits. I haven't seen them before or since, but they are a type I recognise. They could be me, a few years down the road not taken. Mid to late thirties, nine-to-five desk jobs, receding hairlines and six-year engagements, their last vestiges of youth expressed by a vast CD collection and a passion for footie.

One draws the other's attention to someone standing in the next carriage they can see through the doors. The windows are down, so they have to whisper. He says, 'See your man?'

'Which?'

'Your man in the bobble hat.'

'Yeah?'

'Big Roy Keane fan.'

The second guy peers discreetly, says, 'Oh dear.'

'I got sitting in his company one of those mornings just before the

World Cup and your man started laying down the law. I tried to make a few fairly reasonable points about Keane never really wanting to play for Ireland in the first place and the team's record without him. Your man was "wah wah wah wah" this and "wah wah wah wah" that. So eventually I said, "Listen mate, you're obviously the world's leading authority on the subject" and left it at that.'

We start moving again. In the 20 yards of semi-darkness between where we paused and our resting place on the platform, the pre-recorded voice comes over the intercom, saying, 'This train will terminate here.'

83

Roy and Mick have both refused to rule out the possibility of comebacks. Last November, on his last day in charge, FAI chiefs told Mick that his name would be put in the hat next time the Irish manager's post came vacant. Mick was flabbergasted. The FAI even went on to suggest that his name would also be put in the hat the next time after that. Was that part of the settlement deal, that Mick's name would be flagged in perpetuity every time we needed a new manager? Mick eventually gathered himself and said that he would be proud to be considered again for the job, and that if both parties felt a return was really possible then he would certainly consider it.

In this week's *Sunday Times* Roy makes similar noises. He says that when his chinwag with Brian Kerr ended last Friday, the soap opera of his international career had 'To Be Continued' written all over it:

As we were finishing our conversation he said, 'You never know what could happen down the road.' I believe that, still think, 'Never say never.' There are people who placed bets on Roy

Keane never playing for Ireland again: if I were the bookies, I wouldn't pay out just yet. The Champions' League games that Manchester United play mean that it is not feasible just now. What would happen if I was at a club that wasn't playing in Europe? You never know.

In *Ireland on Sunday* of 16 February, there was a little appendix to the report on Roy's reasons for retirement, under the headline 'Are Roy and Mick Heading For a Rematch?' Quinta do Lago in the Algarve is the favourite holiday resort of both. 'The two rivals,' the report states, 'also share a love of the Alto golf club . . . [They] have been desperate to avoid each other since McCarthy sent Keane home from the World Cup and have not spoken since. Now it appears they will be members of the same golf club.' Think about it: a cringing, wordless encounter in an otherwise deserted locker room; Mick defiantly holding his head up and rattling his club unceremoniously; Roy blushing and smiling that smile that suggests he knows something the rest of us don't.

Stan gives a rare interview to the *Irish Independent* in the last week of February. Stan watched the Russia game in a bar in Marbella. 'I felt a loss,' he says, 'a sense of sadness.' He was one of the summarisers on RTÉ radio for the Swiss meltdown, called Mick the next morning and knew the writing was on the wall. And Saipan? The events Stan calls 'one big mess' and the fallout 'a load of codswallop'. He can't seem to remember what Roy is called. 'The person who was involved, if he is honest,' Stan says, 'knows it should never have happened.' Stan and Roy played eleven years together for Ireland. 'The stuff I could tell you about Staunton,' Roy has said. 'And him about me.' That one will no longer bring himself to say the other's name is, it seems to me, as bad as it can get.

By the second week of March Roy's World Cup shenanigans have sufficiently entered the realm of recent history to become the stuff of television quizzes. On the evening of 10 March, in a second-round tie of *University Challenge*, he is the first of three bonus questions worth five points each.

Question: 'Which famous Manchester United footballer once criticised United's home fans for being more interested in eating prawn sandwiches than watching football?'

They confer.

Jeremy Paxman, perhaps experiencing a Dunphy flashback, is getting impatient.

'C'mon . . .'

I am sprawled on the couch, shouting 'I don't believe it, I don't believe it.' and my wife is laughing.

Answer:

'David Beckham?'

'No, that's a terrible guess,' chides Paxman. 'It's obvious: it's Roy Keane.'

That following Saturday, 15 March, he is a multiple-choice worth £1,000 on *Who Wants To Be A Millionaire?*

Question: 'Which player was sent home from the 2002 World Cup?'

Answer Choice: 'A. Michael Owen, B. Thierry Henry, C. Roy Keane, D. A.N. Other.'

The contestant gets it without a flicker of hesitation. I am not in the room when he does. It is an early morning repeat of the midweek show and I am lying in bed. The first I know about it is when Tommy comes bombing up the stairs in his pyjamas shouting,

'Dad, I won £1,000. Dad, wake up, I won £1,000.'

Mick does get the Sunderland job in the second week of March. Howard Wilkinson is surprised to be axed after six successive defeats and two wins in twenty attempts. Even more surprising is the suggestion of the club vice-chairman, John Fickling, that the Roy Keane saga actually swayed the decision in Mick's favour. Mick, Fickling says, came with 'experience'. The manager is less forth-coming on the subject, except to say that he sees his appointment as 'part of the healing process'. Before his first game in charge, at home to Bolton, he is given a hero's ovation when he walks into the Stadium of Light. They lose 2–0.

Within a month Mick has his men playing like Champions' League holders. In the tunnel after another home defeat, this time to Chelsea on 6 April, Claudio Ranieri tells him 'he thought they were playing Real Madrid in the first half'. By the end of the season they have lost Mick's first nine games in charge and are a mere three defeats shy of the all-time league record set by Darwen in 1898/9. They have the lowest points total, the fewest wins and the fewest goals in Premiership history.

'It may sound daft,' Mick tells reporters at the season's end, 'but a lot of people would envy my position.'

Niall Quinn, who acted as coach in the last days of Peter Reid's reign, does not stay on. Instead, Ian Evans, Mick's right-hand man with Ireland, takes his place. There is also a familiar Irish ring to the personnel on the pitch: Jason McAteer, Kevin Kilbane, Thomas Butler, Sean Thornton. By August Mick will have signed Gary Breen, scorer of our second against Saudi Arabia, and Colin Healy, the Corkman whose name was on the official FIFA squad list for twelve hours. It's as if, unable to awake from the nightmare that is his recent history, Mick is gathering his old squad around him for comfort, building his own little offshore enclave: Ireland-upon-Wear.

86

My wife's family has a holiday house in Spiddal, between Galway city and Connemara. We usually go there for a fortnight every summer, and then for the turf fires and damp bed linen of New Year. This year, for the first time, we go at Easter as well and are in residence for the second leg of the Champions' League quarter-final between United and Real. All week the weather has done a pretty passable impersonation of summer. We spend the afternoon of Wednesday, 23 April on the beach. We get sunburned and have chips for tea. Shortly before half seven Tommy and me stroll a mile up the road to the nearest pub.

United are 3–1 down from the first leg. I watched that game behind closed doors at home, and was speechless with disappointment at the final whistle. As a Liverpool fan I am supposed to be thrilled to bits. But Roy has made it clear, perhaps too clear, how much it would mean to him to lift the European Cup. He famously missed the final in 1999, and didn't kick a ball in Japan. This year in particular you know how much pleasure certain analysts and ex-players would take from United's and his elimination.

Spiddal is in the Gaeltacht, one of those small exotic pockets where Irish is spoken in living rooms and across shop counters and even under big screens on Champions' League nights. To make matters stranger the pub is crammed to the rafters with Liverpool fans cheering Real in Irish. Tommy is wearing his Michael Owen jersey and hits the ceiling with the rest of them when Ronaldo scores after just twelve minutes. And though United level it before half-time, and though Beckham does more in the last twelve minutes when it doesn't matter, than he managed in ninety in the Bernebau when it did, the tie is over from that moment. Ronaldo scores a hatrick and gets taken off. His team-mate and Liverpool old boy Steve McManaman is taken off as well and gets a standing ovation from the Spiddal faithful. I suck on three pints and feel like a traitor.

You could count on one hand the amount of touches Roy gets. We are told he is going through a role transition. The old box-to-box, two-footed Roy is gone. The new model reminds me of Tommy on Saturday mornings. He follows the ball to all corners without once putting in the boot. He is the first to the scorer of a United goal and the last to lunge at the ball crossing United's line. *Happiness is not being afraid*? He looks terrified – of spending another month as an injured onlooker, of reading once again about his ubiquitous demons in the morning papers. It is no coincidence that United's league fortunes have been revivified since his return. But these days it's more who he is than what he does. And as soon as a great footballer starts being picked for his 'presence', he's at the top of a long slide to retirement.

I don't have enough Irish to make out what the locals are saying about Roy throughout the game. My guess is it isn't complimentary. Tommy took Mr Roy Keane along for the ride. Before the kick-off one twenty-something chap asked, 'What's her name?'

'It's a him,' Tommy laughed as if the guy was blind.

'What's his name so?'

'Mr Roy Keane.'

The guy turned to his mates and obviously told them, in a flurry of gutturals, that the kid sitting the other side of him had a doll called after Roy. They peered around in unison, gave the moment one collective incredulous shrug and shouted another round. Throughout the rest of the game his name is islanded in sentences I can't decipher. But the fact that it is just 'Keane', not 'Roy' or 'Keano', coupled with their raucous pleasure at Madrid's superiority, seems like a giveaway. Then Roy gets pulled in favour of Fortune with ten minutes plus stoppage left and the pub drops silent. It feels like one of those end-of-an-era moments. I am normally too mortified to utter anything meant to be audible to the rest of a packed pub. I am the one who sits on a high stool down the side and laughs at jokes for general consumption cracked by other people. Roy is halfway to the dugout. The commentator and summariser have put down their mics, the pints are sitting untouched on the tables and counter, and I am already blushing when I shout, 'Go on Roy!'

This is possibly my last chance in civil society. He doesn't play for Ireland any more. At home I am known to shout for United's sworn enemies. I suppose I'm hoping the rest of the punters in the back bar will echo my battle cry, if only out of sentimentality for our greatest warrior. They don't. Instead, I sit there, arms folded and face blazing, staring straight at the telly. It's like being ten again, when you've saved up enough guts to crack a joke in front of the rest of the class and nobody laughs. Tommy says nothing. I can feel him twitching beside me, sipping his Coke with greater frequency than usual and blushing too. I give him a shrug that means to say, 'What the hell.' But he will not meet my eye. Perhaps this is his moment to realise what an embarrassment his old man is. The silence is ended by a few amused mutterings in the background. We polish off our drinks and pull our jackets right side out.

It must hurt even Sir Alex to have to call his man ashore, possibly for the last time on a grandstand European night. Usually no sentimentalist, Sir Alex has gone on record saying that Roy is the greatest he has managed. Now the limbs are in cotton wool, the accelerator doesn't react as quickly as it used to and for the first time in a decade at Old Trafford the mind is distracted by whispers that he is no longer worth his place. A camera flits back and forth from the pitch to his face gazing vacantly on a game in which he has no place and I try to remember a couple of sentences in his book that make approving noises about the manner of Cantona's sudden exit:

> I think he decided that if he couldn't play for United, he wouldn't play at all. I admired that.

I say all this to Tommy on the way home, in the manner of one of those 'there comes a time' father-and-son conversations. We are walking in darkness on a pathless road, wearing luminous armbands. 'But he isn't injured, is he?' is Tommy's only understanding of the situation. I say something about age, about not being able to do things you used to. The words fall on silence and small footsteps beside me. I tell him about our first dog, who lived to thirteen. He was a cairn terrier called Síog (literal translation: 'Fairy' – it was a different age). He was blind in one eye and had one lame paw. One day we came home from school and found him asleep in the garage.

'Roy?'

'No, *Síog*. We found *Síog* asleep in the garage.'

'And did he ever wake up?'

'No. The vet had been that afternoon.'

'And did you get another dog?'

'We did.'

'What did you call him?'

'Síog.'

'You called your second dog Síog as well?'

'We couldn't think of any other name.'

I can make out the outline of his breath when he laughs.

'So you're telling me that after the vet visits Roy, Man United will get another player and call him "Roy Keane"?'

'Hilarious.'

'Beckham was brilliant, Dad, wasn't he?'

Me and my brothers and our generation idolised players our fathers called 'haircuts' or 'puppets'. I figure I can't go on being the crusty bollocks who lays down the law with his son on all things football.

'Yeah, Beckham was brilliant.'

'He should have started, shouldn't he?'

'Yeah, he should have started.'

Reaction to the Real game sees Roy's sell-by-date looming too. 'The sight of Keane retiring nine minutes from time,' Keith Duggan writes in the *Irish Times* of Saturday, 26th April, 'on a gala night for European football was unforgettable. How quickly and intractably an athlete's moment in the sun passes.' Two days later Tom Humphries, the journalist who has interviewed the player so often that McCarthy snarled at the post-Moscow press conference, 'You speak to him on a more regular basis', seems up for drawing a conclusive veil over the whole shebang:

> In the end, he was fine but nothing special. A ghost of himself, tidy and thoughtful and contained. The question is whether he can stand to be that . . . to rage like a furnace when you aren't giving out the old heat . . . Keane has too many enemies and too much pride to make an exhibition of his waning. He could be a defender perhaps but you don't fancy the managing director, the boss of bosses, doing filing just to keep his hand in.

87

Will Roy be remembered as a great footballer? He says no, and he has lots of backers. The argument seems to be based exclusively on the knowledge that he was never a juggler or dribbler. There is, however, a counter argument that reminds us that the taxis of São Paolo and Scarborough are driven by dribblers once tipped for greatness. Roy defines Bryan Robson's greatness as a question of being 'awesome' rather than 'brilliant'. He could just as easily have been talking about himself.

It was never simply that he was Irish, or good. It was more that his way of being good – shyness and courage in equal parts – seemed peculiarly Irish. As a kid he overcame being 'small and shy' through boxing. Years later he would display the boxer's skill of closing off the ring, the balletic art of cornering your man without even throwing a glove, using footwork to narrow the space of an attack. In those moments, he looks like nothing so much as a sheepdog at trials, picking off his sheep one by one.

If there were a milometer attached to those legs, it would have rolled through six noughts several times over. In his young days, drilling into tackles, tearing box to box after lost causes his team-mates had stopped chasing, he looked like a child covering his ears and humming to smother all other unwelcome sounds. He had the happy knack of materialising in open pasture after defences had pushed out and, long-haired, celebrating his goals with the ringside hardcore. In those three seasons from 1998 to 2001, when youthful mania co-existed in perfect equilibrium with mature restraint, he was at his peak, peerless. In Belgrade, November 1999, he played his greatest game in green. You never hear about it, clips are never shown, because it was a game we lost for yet another tournament we didn't grace. Every ball swung into our box came back off his head, every fifty-fifty in the centre circle rebounded off his head, every assault on enemy lines he led. Imagine a hybrid of the Tasmanian Devil and Bobby Charlton.

These days, he knows the aura around his name creates it own space. Head shaved, he waits and holds while the opposition prevaricate over whose turn it is to tackle, then pushes a beautifully weighted pass into the path of younger legs. Long armed and slump shouldered, he hangs back like an eldest brother staying late to lock the family shop. Scarcely will he risk the blushes of something loose and ambitious. Just when the word 'limited' is being muttered all over again, he does something amazing. He skims a 40-yard ball onto a sixpence, or skips past three players into an acre of open space, or scores a peach. Is he the only remaining Premier League player who doesn't obviously practise goal celebrations? Usually, he runs at the crowd and then comes to a sudden stop, arms at his side, looking at his feet, as though embarrassed to find himself in the midst of actions he hasn't thought through.

From that sighting over a decade ago to the friendly against Nigeria last May, he was the one. There have been nights when even those of us who always hated Man United secretly wanted them to win. There have been games for Ireland when, as in Tommy's drawings, he looked like Gulliver. In retrospect, he was surprised and flattered by the tidal wave of affection in the last week of May 2002. So sudden was his exile that he has been denied, and now denied himself, the flattery of retirement, the emotional lap of honour. And that is sad.

88

A local kid has just accepted a three-year contract with Man United, according to a big splash in the 16 May 2003 edition of the *Argus*. Kyle Moran is pictured with his family in their front room. It is an old story. A kid leaves with bunting strung across the street he grew up on and the hopes of a whole neighbourhood on his shoulders. He slips back off the bus three years later, mid-afternoon, with only a backpack crammed with laundry and hard-luck stories. It's difficult not to be pessimistic on his behalf, but that's not fair either. Good luck to him. Perhaps in time his name will surface in a round-up of all the day's other games some Saturday night.

He's sixteen. He has All-Ireland gold medals in high jump, long jump and hurdling. He has pedigree: his grand uncle on his dad's side played for Derby County; his great-grandfather on his mam's, the 'hale and hearty' Harry Holborne, played for Leeds and Man City. He played in one of United's coaching sessions in the area, and caught lots of eyes. He was invited over to train for a week in the Theatre of Dreams, and then again last week. While there he scored a goal, laid claim to all penalties and had the 'natural jauntiness' to go up and speak with Sir Alex. He was even lucky enough to have been around when United finally clinched the title.

As a coda to the article we are told of the great welcome Kyle was granted by current Man United players from this side of the water. Roy Keane was 'a kindly mentor' to him, giving Kyle much of his time and the benefit of his years at the top. 'He was like an uncle to him,' said the lad's father. 'He took him into the canteen for lunch and sat him down and talked seriously to him.' John O'Shea made Kyle's luggage heavier with the gift of his Premiership jersey. Kyle thought John was very tall. But it was Roy Keane, concludes the *Argus*, who 'took an avuncular interest in the local lad, betraying the distant image that he is often portrayed with'. (Literal translation: Roy Keane was surprisingly nice to young Kyle.)

89

Boxing has long been part of Roy's mythology. Whenever there was a dust-up on the pitch someone was bound to say, 'You know he was a boxer, don't you?' You always suspected, however, it was one of those things from the past that got bloated with retelling to bolster a present image, like Dustin Hoffman's track record or Daniel Day Lewis' cabinet-making. His biggest boyhood hero was Mike Tyson. He did join a local club aged nine, but wasn't eligible to fight until he was twelve. So he sparred with his brothers for three years, won four fights in the Irish Novice League and packed it in. 'I was seriously thinking about making a career in the ring,' he once said.

He almost fought several divisions above his weight on the team bus to Logan Airport in Boston, 1992. 'If it hadn't been for Packie Bonner standing in between us,' Mick writes, 'blows may well have been thrown from both sides.' He has since exchanged punches with the best of them in many illustrious tunnels. He got involved on the way to the dressing rooms after a bruiser against Arsenal in February 1997. He rowed in behind Tony Cascarino in Bursa, November 1999, after we had been beaten on an away goal in the play-off for Euro 2000. It was like one of those saloon brawls in an old-fashioned western. The riot police came on, but not in any apparent peace-enforcing role. Roy ended the qualifying campaign, and Tony his international career, in a blizzard of fists. His languid haymaker at Alan Shearer in September 2001 cost him another three games in the wilderness and almost persuaded him to retire.

And we have, you could say, Muhammad Ali to blame for Roy's frame of mind in Saipan the following May. He watched the biopic on the plane over and was moved by one scene in particular. Ali's friends and family are trying to get him to accept conscription for Vietnam, and he is having none of it. They want him to take the soft option, knowing someone of his fame wouldn't really be expected to engage, and he is saying how that went against everything he believed in. 'It's an inspiring notion,' Roy writes, 'a demonstration of conviction that I understand very clearly, and relate to my own life.' However embarrassing it may seem, perhaps Roy landed in Saipan seeing the FAI as the US Government and the World Cup as a 'white man's war' and himself as Ali.

Danny Baker couldn't have known this when he wrote his column for *The Times* of 25 May 2002. But he had a sixth sense of the connection between Ireland's former captain and the former heavyweight champ:

Keane knows more about the World Cup and how football works than almost anybody on the planet. If you just look beyond the happy-sappy Irish squad and on to the bigger picture of why a man would act that way, his actions begin to look almost Ali-like in their honesty.

Then, by sheer coincidence, Roy has to step into Ali's shoes for a few fleeting seconds in June. The occasion is the opening ceremony of the Special Olympics at Croke Park. Ali is guest of honour and, as such, due to pronounce some scripted words to get the ball rolling. Roy is there in suit and tie to lead out the team from China. My friend Mary works backstage that day and tells me later of a sliver of drama at the last minute. Ali, not the man he once was, declares himself unprepared to speak in front of such a huge crowd. So it falls to the next most famous celeb, who happens to be standing in the wings. He is given a piece of paper and pushed onstage to what Mary calls 'a fair old booing'. When it pipes down, Roy reads Ali's lines aloud and walks back off.

The father of one of Tommy's team-mates was there. We discuss it the Saturday morning immediately after.

'It was coming from one particular section of the crowd,' he says. 'It was as if there was a hundred or so people who had hired a couple of coaches and travelled together with the same single intent.'

He can't stand Roy, but he knows I'm a fan. I suggest that there are people out there spending their hard-earned simply for the pleasure of heckling one man. He agrees. He didn't boo himself. Why bother? We shake our heads in unison.

'I thought the way Keane handled the World Cup,' he says, 'was disgraceful. But I never stopped reminding myself what a great player he was for Ireland. There are still people who just will not let it go.'

90

An exchange between my good lady and my heir, overheard the second Saturday of May 2003:

My Wife: 'How did football go today, Tommy?'

Tommy: 'Crap. We lost six-nil.'

My Wife: 'Did you get any goals?'

Tommy: 'Well, hardly!'

He has been going to indoor training all winter in a community hall in a seaside village three miles away. He loves it. Every Saturday morning I drop him and two mates from school. Tommy asked me not to stick around. So I make myself scarce and get back in time for the obligatory end-of-session penalties. You know immediately from his demeanour how it has gone. Will the arms be folded, or will he risk losing his place in the queue to run over and tell me he scored? Now that summer is here it's more serious. The underage league has begun on a piece of reclaimed land down by the docks and a team has been selected from the group.

Tommy is a chip off this old block. He goes through the motions of tracking without shaping to shoulder or actually tackling. He has the vocabulary of football pat, his goal celebrations perfected. As the game drags on and his legs tire, he reverts to honorary life centre forward. He stands at the edge of the opposition's box, hands on hips, calling 'Yes, yes' to a girl taking a throw at the far end of the pitch. Whenever a chance presents itself, he takes three steps back to get his aim and is swamped before he can pull the trigger. The other parents stifle sighs. He looks forward too much to the crisps and juice. He talks about some of his team-mates in tones of utter amazement.

Tommy isn't in the first eleven. His friends aren't either, but they have alibis. One has moved to Wicklow and the other is too old by a month. Tommy isn't entirely alone. In the past few weeks, Eve has joined. Instead of the early shift on Saturdays, we report at noon to the park where the pitches are and hear the teams called out. The selection process is more humane than in his father's day. Everyone gets a jersey and everyone plays. There are two games, but only one counts in league points.

Tommy has yet to realise this. He thinks the games he plays against the subs of the other clubs are for real. He reels off the stats – played, for, against, points – in the passenger seat on the way home after each match. He hasn't noticed the most important stat: that the other simultaneous match is eleven versus eleven for seven-year-olds who look as if they are already shaving; that ours is scraps of unspecified numbers with girls and kids too small for any league. For how much longer? Lately, it has dawned on him that none of the coaches are barking on his touchline. And he doesn't think much of his team-mates. Last week, after consecutive defeats, he asked me, 'Why do we get all the crap players?'

'I'm not with you.'

I was stalling, wondering if I should just come clean.

'The teams the coach is picking are crap.'

'You're on it, so it can't be that bad.'

'Yeah, but why is Evie on it as well when there's much better players they could pick?'

'Ah Tom!'

'I mean it, Dad. I'm going to say it to the coach.'

'I don't think you should.'

I know how he feels. During the winter we were all one big chatty family. Now that the league has kicked off, the parents of the kids on the actual team keep to themselves. The dads wear tracksuits and shout 'Push up, push up'. The mums gossip through the second half. In some instances there are bigger brothers who come along and juggle on the touchline. The league's officials know their names. They belong. We belong with the strays on a bumpier pitch: the settled hippies like ourselves; the yuppies whose kid is called something like 'Otto', who tog out *en famille* and cheer too much; the single mothers who watch from the car park and get reminders about the annual voluntary donation. Now that the league has kicked off, you pass one of the parents of the first eleven in the shopping centre and they blank you.

Tommy tells me that when he is big he will play for Dundalk and Liverpool and Ireland, all at once. I stay silent. I think my son is lucky. The worst that can happen is that his heart will be broken for a while. When he gets over it, as we all did, he'll still be clever, handsome, funny. Football chooses only a few. The really *un*lucky ones are those almost good enough, whose lives football ruins. Dunphy is brilliant on this in *Only a Game?* He talks with great honesty and compassion about the nineteen-year-olds who get their hopes raised and then are dropped, unsigned and uneducated, into the real world. Roy was almost one of those. A psychologist in the Channel 4 documentary, *Inside the Mind of Roy Keane*, suggests that he has been haunted by that knowledge throughout his professional career, that his fabled desire to win is as much a fear of failure. And fear of failure, says the psychologist, is a known source of the blues.

91

When Roy first joined United the club's training pitch was called The Cliff. Shacked up for a week in the Four Season's Hotel, Britain's most expensive footballer was so terrified of being late for his first training session that he got there an hour early. In one of three extraordinary sentences in his autobiography that seem overshadowed by death, he remembers:

I ordered a taxi, told the driver to lead the way to The Cliff and followed in my car.

Another alludes bewilderingly to 'three of [his] closest school friends, all of whom are now dead'. A third rounds off a longish passage of self-disgust after an account of his sending off against Newcastle in September 2001: the red mist when defeat is on the cards, the attempt to send Alan Shearer into orbit, and the silent bus ride back to Manchester in darkness with all his past misdemeanours being replayed in his head. As the players are heading for their respective cars, the manager says goodnight and Keane can scarcely mumble a reply. Sensing the turmoil of the player's state of mind, Ferguson says, 'Don't do anything stupid, Roy.'

That the manager hadn't given the captain a bollocking that afternoon is a fair indication of one's understanding of the black space towards which the other gravitates. Perhaps even more interesting than the choice of words is the choice of the author to repeat the story, potentially to his own detriment. He is too pathologically private, and Dunphy has too much nous about the balance of reticence and revelation that makes a sports star's life story interesting, to come straight out and write: 'I am battling the booze, and sometimes I feel like hanging myself.' Or is it that Roy, like Cantona, is deliberately manipulating his own mythology and sniggering on the other side of the uncorrected proofs?

Two days before the match in Cyprus in which Roy won his fiftieth cap in March 2001, Mick McCarthy's father died. Mick was on his way back to England when he heard about the provocative interview Roy had done with the *Sunday Independent*. When the Iranian national coach, Miroslav Blazevic, arrived in Dublin that November, it was with dire suicidal warnings. Blazevic had taken Croatia to the semi-final of France 1998 and stepped aside after their Euro 2000 qualification campaign failed, thanks to ourselves and Yugoslavia. We were well used to his old flannel. He told reporters in Dublin that if Iran lost, he would hang himself from the goalposts after the second leg in Tehran.

Saipan has been a US trust territory, with identical status to other trust territories such as Puerto Rico, since its invasion by American troops in June 1944. It was from the next island down, Tinian, that the Enola Gay took off bound for Hiroshima in August 1945. To this day Tinian has the eerie distinction of being home to the longest runway in the world. The rumours of terror that preceded the Americans prompted the native population of Saipan to embark on a mass collective suicide. They gathered at a cliff and the youngest went first. And so on, until the last eldest male of each family stepped backwards over the edge. The Marines set up a PA system to broadcast persuasive pleas in English. It was useless. Twenty-two thousand civilians died, the vast majority of those by their own hands. Today, Suicide Cliff is the island's biggest tourist attraction.

Roy spoke about it towards the end of his infamous interview with Tom Humphries, the day before he was expelled from the squad. He described a guided tour the team was given, his interest in the history of the place. As a chilling coda to that scenic route, he said:

I was going to go back up there today to that cliff! Add an Irishman to the list (laughs).

There is something about Roy that makes us instinctively take the laugh, and not the words, with a pinch of salt. Not to suggest that there was ever any possibility of his jumping off a cliff into the Pacific. But over the years sympathisers and detractors alike have made reference to his self-destruct impulse. One Irish player who went to see him the night after the fatal team meeting, likened his ex-captain's high spirits to 'a fella on Death Row, talking about the good meal you get'.

That weekend, many journalists found it impossible to resist the unhappy coincidence of Saipan's history and Roy's fatalistic disposition. 'The feel-good factor is over,' wrote Katherine Holmquist in the *Irish Times*. 'Depression starts here . . . we will never be as optimistic again.' Philip Quinn took a more predictable route in the *Irish Independent* when he likened Roy's actions to hara kiri, and argued that 'short of taking a running jump off the nearby suicide cliffs . . . Keane couldn't have opted for a more dramatic departure from the stage he has graced for a decade.' Tommy Conlon, in a witty and moving opinion piece for the *Sunday Independent*, described that nervousness about Roy's well-being many Irish fans experienced in the season preceding Korea/Japan and the 'pall of bad karma hanging in the air':

> It seemed as if Keane had some sort of World Cup death wish that had been festering long before he flew out with the squad nine days ago.

Brian Clough chose similarly destructive terms to criticise his ex-player, telling one newspaper that he would have 'shot him' before he left the room. 'Come to think of it, I wouldn't have needed to have shot him,' Old Big Head backtracked, 'because he's shot himself.' On the team bus from the Saipan Hyatt to the airport the back row seat on which the captain usually sat was empty, but for an envelope with the letters RIP written on it. Most of the light-hearted sightings from the team plane were of someone inching back to the cliffs to end it all. 'Nobody died,' the man himself had tried to tell Tom Humphries. Yet John Fallon, the squad kitman, says that 'it was like a funeral' and 23 May was treated by many at home like a national day of grief. Paddy Power, Ireland's leading bookmaker, declared himself 'in mourning' and someone else left a condolence wreath on the steps of the FAI. Jason McAteer had to be included on the police watch list as a result of his behaviour towards Roy in the Stadium of Light at the other end of his summer. He recently revealed:

> I knew it would get nasty afterwards and it did. I got three death threats from United fans, an envelope containing white powder and a message that said I was dead.

We are peerless when it comes to bearing grudges. Sojourn in an Irishman's bad books can last decades, and as long as it does you might as well not exist. None of Ireland's World Cup squad, nor any of the staff or management, have heard from Roy Keane since May 2002. Niall Quinn told Roy, when he went to the room with Stan, that they might never meet again. They did exchange a passing handshake at Sunderland. 'It's been three months of shit, Roy,' Niall tried to say. 'Enough is enough.' Roy didn't answer and hasn't been in touch. Roy never answered any of the text messages sent to him by John Fallon. He and Fallon had become almost close until Saipan. 'I haven't spoken to him since,' Fallon says. 'It's shocking.' It's as if, to Roy, they no longer exist.

92

> I just think it's farcical they way it's still brought up every day of the week . . . And it will be for the rest of our lives probably.
> Steven Staunton, *Irish Independent*, 24 February, 2003

In the future, Irish fans will pay pilgrimage to the sweatshops of Saipan, much as the trenches of Flanders became a tourist attraction in the early 1920s, to lay wreaths and stand in moments of silent emotional prayer. The new national manager, Lee Carsley, will be found murdered in his bed. Gardaí will believe the weapon to have been an extremely blunt instrument, possibly even a rag doll. Fuzzy closed-circuit footage from the foyer of Carsley's apartment block will show a man in his mid-thirties and a boy aged nine or ten, but the case will never be solved.

Stan Staunton, the footballer turned chat show host, will campaign tirelessly for the canonisation of his late friend, Niall Quinn. Quinn's widow, Gillian, will see out her career as the golden-hearted landlady of The Woolpack in *Emmerdale*. The tracks between her and her past will be covered in the credits by the surname of her late second husband, Pat Kenny. Mick McCarthy, a retired greenkeeper in the Algarve whom members rumour to have had a colourful life, will be visited in old age by a trickle of oral historians. Mohammad Keano, the author of several bestselling self-help books for men, including *Without a Doubt, Apologising is Poison* and *Succeed to Prepare, Prepare to Succeed*, will collapse and pass away on the grounds of his Boston home while playing hide-and-seek with his grandson whom he affectionately calls 'The Gaffer'.

On 22 May of every year the older teachers will feel it important to remind their pupils why they are getting the next day off. On the public holiday newsreaders and civic leaders will wear floral head-dress as a mark of remembrance, the last surviving members of the Irish squad will march at exactly 7.30pm to the statue of the Unknown Penalty-Taker and a lone bugler will play 'Stand By Me'. Our idea of time will eventually be divided by those years before and those years after Genesis, the way the Julian calendar adheres to the birth of Christ. Some historically literate wag, sifting through a trad archive, will happen upon an unnamed polka and christen it 'The Humours of Roy'. And for generations to come, wherever green is worn and whenever the acronym FAI is uttered, the words 'piss-up' and 'brewery' will mysteriously spring to mind.

93

On the first anniversary of Saipan, Friday, 23 May 2003, Dean Kiely, the reserve keeper who had cracked a lame joke about filling Roy's boots in the deathly silence of the Hyatt ballroom, puts on the souvenir T-shirt he bought at Coral Ocean Point and plays eighteen holes. In the *Sunday Independent* of 25 May, Kiely says he would be slow to call his round commemorative, yet the combination of occasion and its marking seems too apposite to be coincidence.

'What happened out there was out-of-the-ordinary,' he says. 'I made the joke at the time and it showed a bit of comic timing, but it hasn't led to any after-dinner offers.'

Roy has taken up yoga. The energy that fuels his rage could float the national grid over Christmas and New Year. Presumably, he is hoping to redirect that energy to more positive ends and to improve his disciplinary record. In the last week of May a club spokesman tells the *Sun*, 'It may seem unlikely but Roy is loving his yoga. Maybe he has found inner peace.'

Epilogue

That's it. That's the story. At times you are loath to admit as much, in case some further minor twist breathes new life into it. But in truth, everything that happens after this point is not a new chapter but rather belongs to another story entirely. The rest is mere opinion – self-justifying, vaguely sickening and way past its sell-by date – and we have all had too much of that.

If we can get beyond the rights and wrongs, the rote apportioning of disgrace, we are left with a uniquely interesting case in which football's stock-in-trade patriotism gets exposed for the bluster it mostly is. I don't doubt that being Irish means a great deal to Roy Keane, but there is lots of evidence that by May 2002 playing for Ireland – 'a strange experience' that became 'a nuisance' – was something he undertook only to satisfy his family's understandable pride. Probably friendless within the Irish set-up, possibly recovering from alcoholism of which the Irish manager must have been aware, by his own admission he 'dreaded the prospect of international week'.

And Mick? Let's give him the benefit of the doubt, and say that he found himself at the centre of a hurricane that was largely not of his making. Only a mug would believe that to be the whole truth, but at least that half-truth lets the sleeping dog 'Saipan' sleep on. Without a sliver of sarcasm, I would love to hear Mick on his current sense of Irishness. The man who admits he cheered England as a kid in 1966, who captained his father's country to its first World Cup, who managed it during its most recent World Cup and within six months had become the patsy for an association in turmoil – how Irish does Mick feel now? Seriously, I'd love to know.

Let's just say it wasn't to be and leave it there. Roy and Mick were on a collision course from long ago. By the end of May 2002, neither was prepared to allow the other the satisfaction of a World Cup. There are still conspiracy theorists out there, such as our postman, who consider Saipan the clearing in the woods into which Mick McCarthy lured his captain. Last week an intelligent, sentient person confessed to me his fantasy of smashing Roy Keane's head with a sledgehammer. Saipan, if you like, was the ultimate score draw of the Charlton/McCarthy era. Roy, at the World Cup on the reluctant sufferance of his club, lost his international career. The second he stepped from the ballroom of the Hyatt Hotel it was over. Mick lost his job and for months looked like a man in recovery after treading on a landmine. They cancelled each other out. It finished 1–1.

In July 2003 Her Majesty the Queen awards Niall Quinn an honorary MBE for services to football and charitable causes. He and Gillian are building their dream home in the horsey heartland of Naas, Co. Kildare. At the beginning of the new season Steve Staunton moves on a free transfer from Aston Villa to, fittingly, Coventry. Roy, on Eamon Dunphy's new chat show the night before Ireland's fatal final Euro 2004 qualifier in Basle, expresses regret at their falling out. 'I have some time for Stan,' he says, which is praise indeed by Mayfield standards.

Sunderland do not, however, equal or surpass the 104-year record still held by the Victorians of Darwen. After losing the first two games of the new season and bringing their total of straight
ts to seventeen, they beat Preston on 24 August. In his elation,
ds his true age. 'I've met the lads from Darwen,' Mick
s, 'and told them they can keep it.' His team wins
two of their next eleven games. At the time of
urth in Division One, looking like promotion
ing some real football. Jason McAteer, the
club captain, is no longer concerned that his
the past.

'I class Mick McCarthy as a friend as well,' Jason says. 'We had a good chat over a beer the other week and he understands that times have moved on.'

Roy spends the summer of 2003 studying for coaching badges. He starts the new season playing like a two-year-old and proves all prophesies of doom to have been, for the time being, premature. 'When was the last time you saw the guy look happy?' Niall asks accusingly in his autobiography. These days, unburdened of the weight of international duty, Roy looks happier than he has in years, and that's as it should be. Word is, he and Mick Byrne, the former Irish assistant physio who acted as his go-between with McCarthy, have met and patched things up. The yoga is working. His attempts at peacemaker in the brawl that concludes the home game with Arsenal are widely praised. He plays at Ibrox in the Champions' League and seems to revel in the deafening boos that follow his every touch. He even scores a few. We mention each in passing in the pub. We fold our arms and half smile, careful not to seem too pleased since these days he is just a United player.

'And Roy scored.'

'Yeah, Roy scored.'

'Good goal, too.'

'Not bad.'

'Not bad at all.'

He scores an 82-minute winner at Elland Road on 18 October. At the end of the game he and Gary Kelly share what Cathal Dervan calls in the *Star* 'a warm handshake and an embrace approaching a hug'. Kelly is the player said to have initiated the applause for McCarthy after the infamous squad meeting. Dervan writes:

It was heartening to see such generosity of spirit from two men diametrically opposed in the World Cup war that engulfed the summer of 2002.

Mr Roy Keane remains one of the main gang on Tommy's pillow. Although his yellow hair has begun shedding and he bears the scars of a scrap with a King Charles spaniel from four doors down, he is still smiling. Tommy has started tagging along the odd Saturday lunchtime and cheers loudest in the front bar when Liverpool score. He buys me, with his mother's help, an official Ireland jersey for my birthday. We wear them watching the Switzerland game and are both genuinely heartbroken. Halfway through the second half, Tommy asks out of the blue, 'Dad, what position is "left outside"?'

He is, however, picked for the last but one actual league game of the summer. Several of the first-choice players are on holiday and Tommy finds himself off the pace in the first half. 1–1. During the switch of ends it starts to drizzle. My wife and daughter pull their jackets over their hair and say they'll see us at home. Tommy is pushed up from sweeper to midfield. He is unrecognisable. He flings himself into a couple of tackles. He hits the side netting. He has a goal disallowed. Two opposition mothers to my right point and say, '*He's* good.'

Then *he* scores. A shot from the edge of the box and a big cheer along the touchline. It is allowed. I watch in shock as he covers his head with the luminous bib and is mobbed by his team-mates. 2–1. On the path home, Tommy in his studs and his old man in a saturated T-shirt, I keep repeating the same thing, 'You scored.'

'I know.'

The way he says it, smiling, it's as if he is the one who has known a secret for some time and has been waiting for me to hear it elsewhere, not the other way around.

'You scored,' I say. 'In the league.'

'I know,' he says. 'I know.'

Acknowledgements

Several books address themselves in part to this subject. They are: *Roy Keane: The Autobiography*, Roy Keane with Eamon Dunphy (Michael Joseph, 2002); *Niall Quinn: The Autobiography*, Niall Quinn (Headline, 2002); *Ireland's World Cup 2002*, Mick McCarthy with Cathal Dervan (Simon & Schuster/TownHouse, 2002); *The Gaffers: Mick McCarthy, Roy Keane and the Team They Built*, Paul Howard (O'Brien Press, 2002); *Laptop Dancing and the Nanny Goat Mambo: A Sportswriter's Year*, Tom Humphries (Pocket/Town-House, 2003); *Beyond the Green Door*, Brendan Menton (Blackwater Press, 2003). Other book sources include: *Roy Keane: The Biography*, Tim Ewbank and Stafford Hildred (revised edition, John Blake, 2002); *There's Only One Keano*, Mark Evans (Marino Books, 1999); *The Little Book of Keane*, by 'The Unknown Fan' (New Island Books, 2002); *Full Time: The Secret Life of Tony Cascarino*, Tony Cascarino with Paul Kimmage (Simon & Schuster/TownHouse, 2000); *Captain Fantastic: My Football Career and World Cup Experience*, Mick McCarthy with Matthew Nugent (O'Brien Press, 1990); *Ooh Aah Paul McGrath: The Black Pearl of Inchicore*, Paul McGrath with Cathal Dervan (Mainstream Publishing, 1994); *Gazza Agonistes*, Ian Hamilton (revised edition, Bloomsbury 1998); *Psycho*, Stuart Pearce (Headline, 2000); *Futebol: The Brazilian Way of Life*, Alex Bellos (Bloomsbury, 2002); *Jack & Bobby: A Story of Brothers in Conflict*, Leo McKinstry (CollinsWillow, 2002); *Brilliant Orange: The Neurotic Genius of Dutch Football*, David Winner (Bloomsbury, 2000); *Only a Game?*, Eamon Dunphy (Viking, 1976). I am indebted also to *Have Boots, Will Travel* (RTÉ Television, 1997); *Roy Keane: As I See It* (Odyssey Entertainments, 2002); and *Inside the Mind of Roy Keane* (Channel 4, 2003).

Versions of some of the sections of this book originally appeared in *The Dublin Review* (number 9, Winter 2002/3) under the title 'One-One'. Thanks to its editor, Brendan Barrington. Thanks also to: Cormac Kinsella, Peter Straus, Bill Swainson, Paul Durcan, Bríd Ní Chuillinn and Gerard Fanning, Tony O'Donoghue, John Courtney, Andy Needham, Declan Lynch, Tommy Gorman, Sarah Searson, Mary Hickson, Tony Flynn, John Brown, the extended Groarke family for being such good sports, Frank Daly, Joan O'Callaghan, my four brothers, Tommy O'Callaghan, Eve O'Callaghan and, especially, Vona Groarke for simulating interest so well and so long.

A NOTE ON THE AUTHOR

Conor O'Callaghan is the author of two acclaimed poetry collections, *The History of Rain* (shortlisted for the Forward Poetry Prize Best First Collection and winner of the Patrick Kavanagh Award) and *Seatown*. He lives in Co. Louth, Republic of Ireland, with his wife and fellow poet Vona Groarke, and their two children, Tommy and Eve.

A NOTE ON THE TYPE

The text of this book is set in Bembo. This type was first used in 1495 by the Venetian printer Aldus Manutius for Cardinal Bembo's *De Aetna*, and was cut for Manutius by Francesco Griffo. It was one of the types used by Claude Garamond (1480–1561) as a model for his Romain de L'Université, and so it was the forerunner of what became standard European type for the following two centuries. Its modern form follows the original types and was designed for Monotype in 1929.